GRAN CANARIA
POCKET GUIDE

STEAKS 📍100 m

DIAMANT Restaurant

BROOKLAWN 100 m

JOE'S BURGERS Restaurant

ARTS & CULTURE

Space disc featuring

A TO Z INFO

SHOPPI

Shopping arou be

GATE BRIDGE 📍100 m

🔗 SHARE

📍 MAP

❤ LIKE

Sailing under the Golden Gate Bridge today, it is interesting to consider that engineers once thought it impossible to span the Golden Gate Strait at this point, because of the depth of the water (318ft/ 97 meters, at its deepest point) and the powerful tidal rush.

The city authorized studies for a bridge in 1917, but it was 1933 before the first shovel turned under the gaze of master engineer Joseph B. Strauss (no relation to the famous waltz composer). Four years later the bridge opened, at a cost of $35 million and the lives of 11 construction workers. Today the bridge

INSIGHT ⊘ GUIDES
SPAIN

☰ INTRODUCTION

📄 EXPLOR

FLORIDA 🛒 $8.00

This new edition of Insight Guide Florida is packed with full-colour travel guide photos with inspiration and pictures. It has everything on everything from coastal surf lives and

FRANCE 🛒 $8.00

This brand new edition Insight Guide to France features outstanding edition packed with full-colour photos combining over 750 brand new photographs and inspiring explorations of all the places to go.

FRANCE 🛒 $8.00

ST LUCIA Pocket Guide 🛒 $8.00

St Lucia is one of the most Lucian's dream islands, more so is dramatic than islands. Be inspired. It is lively by Insight's brand new Pocket Guide St Lucia, with full-colour guide.

🛒 $8.00

Walking Eye
mobile app

Discover the world's best destinations with the Insight Guides Walking Eye app, available to download for free in the App Store and Google Play.

The container app provides easy access to fantastic free content on events and activities taking place in your current location or chosen destination, with the possibility of booking, as well as the regularly-updated Insight Guides travel blog: Inspire Me. In addition, you can purchase curated, premium destination guides through the app, which feature local highlights, hotel, bar, restaurant and shopping listings, an A to Z of practical information and more. Or purchase and download Insight Guides eBooks straight to your device.

TOP 10 ATTRACTIONS

ROQUE NUBLO
The towering monolith is a symbol of Gran Canaria. See page 76.

PLAYA DE LAS CANTERAS
This lively city beach is popular with local people and tourists alike. See page 38.

CRUZ DE TEJEDA
Marks one of the highest points on the island. See page 75.

BARRANCO DE GUAYADEQUE
It is easy to drive through this beautiful valley. See page 45.

MASPALOMAS
Its pristine dunes are like a desert by the sea. See page 53.

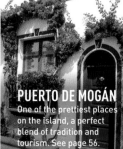

PUERTO DE MOGÁN
One of the prettiest places on the island, a perfect blend of tradition and tourism. See page 56.

CENOBIO DE VALERÓN
The most impressive pre-Hispanic granary on the island. See page 68.

CASA DE COLÓN
One of the finest traditional buildings in Las Palmas, it is claimed Columbus once stayed here. See page 33.

TEROR
A pretty town with a long history. See page 72.

MIRADOR DEL BALCÓN
Enjoy a break from the demanding west coast road at this stunning viewpoint. See page 62.

A PERFECT DAY

9.00am

Las Palmas: breakfast

Have breakfast beneath the trees at a table outside the pretty little Art Nouveau kiosk in Parque San Telmo.

12 noon

Pueblo Canario

Take a bus or taxi to leafy Parque Doramas to admire the splendour of the Hotel Santa Catalina and visit the Pueblo Canario, a beautifully designed complex of traditional island buildings and a museum that pays homage to artist Néstor, one of the brothers who designed the complex.

11.00am

Casa de Colón

Visit the Casa de Colón to admire the beautiful latticed balconies and the replica of a cabin from one of Columbus' ships.

1.30pm

Lunch

Take a taxi to Parque Santa Catalina, where elderly men play chess beneath the palms, and horse-drawn carriages await passengers. After wandering through, stop for a light lunch at 100 Montaditos (tel: 902 197 494) by the port on Muelle Santa Catalina. It's a *cerveceria*, which means the beer will be good.

10.00am

City view

For a panoramic view of the city, take the lift that whizzes you up to the rooftop of the Catedral de Santa Ana. When you've drunk in the vistas, visit the cathedral itself to enjoy the peace in the delightful cloister.

Playa de las Canteras

Head across the narrow neck of the peninsula to Playa de las Canteras for a swim in the warm shallow water, protected by a reef called La Barra. Soak up some sun on the sands, then stroll along the lively promenade until you reach the prestigious Auditorio Alfredo Kraus, home to the Las Palmas Philharmonic Orchestra.

useo Elder

travelling with
ildren the Museo
der is a must-do. Even
you are not, you will
fascinated by this
novative science and
chnology museum in
building that belonged
the Elder-Dempster
ipping Line in the
ys when Britain
actically colonised the
and.

Aperitif time

When you are ready
to head out for the
evening, make your
way to Plazoleta de
Cairasco where you
can check out what
exhibitions are on at the
cultural centre known
as CICCA, then have an
aperitif in the elegant
square while you watch
the sun go down.

Dinner

It is not too far to walk
to Deliciosa Marta (see
page 106), in Calle Pérez
Galdós, an excellent
restaurant serving one
of the finest food in
town. And if you still
have some energy, and
enjoy live music, head to
La Guarida del Blues in
Calle Portugal 68, which
keeps going until late.

CONTENTS

INTRODUCTION

The Canary Islands have always been regarded as a bridge between continents. They were the last stopping-off point for Columbus on his journey of discovery in 1492, when emergency repairs were done in Las Palmas to one of his three ships. During the 16th and 17th centuries, the islands were important trading centres through which passed much of the profitable sea traffic between Spain and the Americas. Latin American influences are still visible in the food and the language, while the architecture reminds us that these were Spanish colonies at a time when the peninsula was at its most wealthy and powerful.

The archipelago lies in the Atlantic Ocean, some 1,100km (700 miles) southwest of mainland Spain and comprises the islands of Gran Canaria, Lanzarote and Fuerteventura to the east, and Tenerife, La Gomera, La Palma and El Hierro to the west. Gran Canaria, the third largest island, is some 195km (120 miles) from the African mainland, on a level with southern Morocco, and covers an area of 1,532 sq km (592 sq miles).

LANDSCAPE, WILDLIFE AND CLIMATE

Gran Canaria was formed some 16 million years ago by volcanic activity beneath the Atlantic, at a point where continental drift made the ocean bed particularly unstable. The central mountain massif was once a volcano, and the gorges (*barrancos*) radiating from it were formed by the subsequent process of erosion. Although the island is so small, it is extremely diverse. The eastern side is lush and fertile; the north and west somewhat bleak and barren; while the stretches of white sand dunes in the south, barely populated until the 1960s, are now the island's holiday playground. Coastal roads in the west are winding and vertiginous, with stunning views, while away from the coast, all roads lead upwards. The highest point is the Pico de las Nieves – Peak of the Snows – at 1,949m (6,394ft).

Vegetation on Gran Canaria is as varied as the landscape. The fire-resistant Canary pine *(Pinus canariensis)* rules over the mountainous zone, while a pink rock rose *(Cistus symphytifolius)* clusters around its feet, and varieties of thyme, sage and broom scent the air. The Canary Island spurge *(Euphorbia canariensis)* survives well in the dry southern region, while southern valleys support verdant groves of date palms *(Phoenix canariensis)*. The most unusual vegetation is the dragon tree *(Dracaena draco)*, which got its name from its red resin known as

Hundreds of plant species are endemic to the Canary Islands

dragon's blood; this ancient survivor is mostly seen in botanical gardens. The plants you notice immediately – brilliant bougainvillaea, hibiscus and poinsettia, clambering over walls and brightening parks and gardens – are not indigenous but were brought to the islands from subtropical parts and have flourished in the equable climate.

Island birds include the indigenous blue chaffinch *(pinzón* in Spanish); greenfinches – not indigenous but very happy here – greater-spotted woodpeckers in the pine forests; the shy Canary chat; and canaries.

Gran Canaria has year-round sunshine – some 300 days a year in the south. A strange grey haze called the *panza de burro* – donkey's belly – sometimes affects the north. Winter

Carnival cheer

Carnival began as a religious event, a last celebration before the lean days of Lent, and developed into a riotous affair, with lavish processions and costumed balls. Carnival takes place throughout the Catholic world and the major ones in Gran Canaria and Tenerife are usually staggered so they do not take place at exactly the same time.

temperatures average 22–24°C (72–75°F), summer averages are 26–28°C (79–82°F), but they often exceed 30°C (86°F). High season is November to April, but July and August are also popular with Spanish visitors and with English and German families, taking advantage of long school holidays.

PEOPLE AND LANGUAGE

Gran Canaria is part of the Spanish Autonomous Region of the Canary Islands. The population numbers 847,000, of whom over 383,000 live in the capital, Las Palmas. They are, on the whole, relaxed, open-minded people, but keen to stress that they are *canarios*, first and foremost. Mainland Spaniards they refer to as *'los peninsulares'*.

Spanish *(castellano)* is the language of the islands. However, there are differences from the peninsula, many of which reflect the two-way traffic between the Canaries and Latin America. A number of Latino words have been borrowed: a bus is a *guagua* and potatoes are *papas*. The strong English influence on the islands has also left some linguistic traces: a cake is a *queque*, and a traditional Canarian knife is a *naife*.

There is a large expatriate population – chiefly English and German – many of whom came initially for holidays. The official religion is Catholic, although Anglican, Muslim, Mormon and other religions have a presence.

Most of the numerous traditional festivals on the island have religious origins. The wild pre-lent carnival stands out but there are other fascinating ones, including the fiesta of the

Virgen del Carmen, when the patron saint of the sea is honoured in the majority of ports and the Bajada de las Ramas in Puerto de las Nieves.

ECONOMY AND ENVIRONMENT

Traditionally, the island's economy has been dependent on agriculture, from sugar cane in the 16th century to cochineal, bananas and tomatoes. The principal source of employment today is in the service sector, of which tourism is a major part. EU funds have been used to strengthen the island infrastructure. There are plans for a rail line between Las Palmas and Playa del Inglés, but at the time of writing work has not yet started. The island suffers from a water shortage, which is intensified by the strain so many visitors place on the system, but this has been partly overcome by the creation of desalination plants, some fuelled by wind power.

Palm Sunday procession in Teror

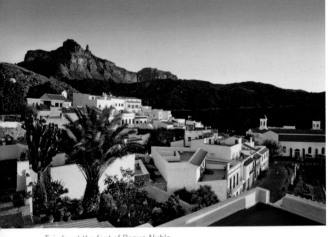
Tejeda, at the foot of Roque Nublo

In an attempt to break away from the sun, sand and sangria image of the islands, a large amount has also gone into the *turismo rural* initiative, whereby traditional buildings are converted into rural hotels in areas of great natural beauty,

REASONS TO VISIT

Although many people visit Gran Canaria for the sun and sand, there is a great deal more on offer. Las Palmas is a true capital city with a vibrant cultural life. There is a splendid auditorium, three theatres, a cultural centre with a varied programme, some excellent restaurants, lively nightlife in the clubs and bars, and numerous good museums. The northern towns of Arucas and Teror have delightful historic centres with traditional architecture. The *barrancos* (gorges) are lush with tropical vegetation. The south is ideal for boating and water sports of all kinds, with craft and equipment available for hire; and, a short distance from the brash resorts, the vast and empty dunes of Maspalomas feel like a desert by the sea.

A BRIEF HISTORY

Much of the Canary Islands' history between their conquest in the late 15th-century and the present is tied up with that of the Spanish mainland. As a vital point for trade with the Americas, Gran Canaria briefly shared in the prosperity of Spain's Golden Age, although it suffered economic decline thereafter. And in the late 20th century, the islands, along with Spain, became part of the European Union. But long before the Spaniards ever set foot here, there was a flourishing civilisation.

LAND OF THE BRAVE

Tamarán – land of the brave – was the proud name given to Gran Canaria by the Guanches, the pre-Hispanic people of the islands. No one is quite sure where the Guanches came from. Some historians and scientists think they were related to the Canarii tribe, who lived on the Saharan side of the Atlas Mountains. The few fragments of writing that can be reconstructed are similar to scripts used by the ancient Berber people, and some Canarian place names are similar too. But as far as can be deduced, the Guanches had no boats, so how they crossed from the African coast remains a mystery. Perhaps, having settled on the islands, they simply forgot how to sail.

Guanche skulls in the Museo Canario, Las Palmas

Quite a lot has been discovered about the culture of these original islanders. Language and social structure varied from island to island. On Gran Canaria, the rulers were called *guanartemes* and shared some of their power with a *faycan*, who combined the role of judge and priest. Next on the social ladder came the aristocracy, the *guayres*.

The Guanches were a settled, agricultural people, who lived in groups of caves. *Gofio*, toasted flour originally made from barley, was their staple, but they also ate a variety of roots, wild fruits and berries. Pigs, sheep and goats provided meat as well as the materials for shelters, containers and clothes, and milk also came from sheep and goats. Fish formed a part of their diet, even when they had to travel some distance down to the coast to find it.

The Guanches did not have the wheel, they knew nothing of metalworking and did not use bows and arrows. Their domestic implements were made from stone and bone or from obsidian, a black, volcanic glass. Porous lava was made

The Canary Islands as seen on the 14th-century Catalan Atlas

into millstones and mortars. Their vessels and containers were made from pottery, wood, leather and woven cane. They mummified their dead and buried them in caves or stone-lined graves, and it is evidence from mummies so far discovered that has led scientists to place the original islanders' ethnic origins in northwest Africa. The Museo Canario has a number of mummies and skulls in its collection, along with domestic items, remarkably well preserved in the dry climate.

THE CONQUERORS ARRIVE

The first conquering force, in 1403, was led by a Norman lord, Jean de Béthencourt, and funded by the king of Castile, but he failed to take the two main prizes – Gran Canaria and Tenerife. It wasn't until 1478 that another attempt was made, under the aegis of the Catholic Monarchs – Ferdinand and Isabella – of a newly united Spain. As the force was under-manned and the indigenous people put up quite a fight, it took several years to subdue them. Pedro de Vera was the man for the job. Arriving as military governor in 1480 he is said to have killed Doramas, the most warlike of the chiefs, with his own hands on the Montaña de Arucas. This coup, and the capture and conversion two years later of chief Tenesor Semidan brought the native people under control, but not before many of them had been killed, starved to death or committed ritual suicide.

De Vera remained governor for 10 years, during which time, in the interests of security, he had many of the local population deported or enslaved. This, together with an influx of European farmers and entrepreneurs, plus two severe out-breaks of plague, meant that within half a century the indigenous population was outnumbered. Those who survived had been forcibly 'converted' and many had inter-married with the incomers.

PROSPERITY AND DECLINE

Because of their location, the Canary Islands became a proving ground for future Spanish colonisation strategies in the Americas. These revolved around slavery and sugar cane, both of which were introduced to the Americas from the Canaries. The sugar boom on the Canaries only lasted until the mid-16th century, when competition from Brazil and the Caribbean became too strong. While Tenerife was able to switch to a lucrative wine industry, conditions on Gran Canaria were unsuitable for viniculture and the island became something of a poor relation, locked in fierce rivalry with flourishing Tenerife, which became the residence of the Captain-General and location of the first university.

The problems Gran Canaria suffered during the 16th and 17th centuries were intensified by the fact that the island and her ships were frequently attacked by pirates. The worst outrage was in 1599, when the Dutch buccaneer Pieter van der Does sacked and burned Las Palmas.

Gran Canaria began to assert its independence – from Tenerife and mainland Spain – in 1808 when the Napoleonic Wars destroyed Tenerife's wine trade. A junta was formed in Las Palmas, calling for 'a patriotic government, independent of the peninsula', but it was unsuccessful. Not until the 1860s did the island's fortunes begin to recover, with the introduction of cochineal, the red dye produced from a beetle of the same name that feeds on cacti. The boom was short-lived, as the invention

Pirate attack

The Bishop's Palace in Las Palmas was one notable victim of van der Does' attack; another was the capital's Catedral de Santa Ana. In a display case in the cathedral today there is a splendid bell, a gift from the Asociación Nederlandesa-Canaria in 1999, 500 years after the privateer destroyed the original.

Gran Canaria suffered many pirate attacks in the 17th century.

of cheaply produced aniline dyes brought a virtual end to the industry. Poverty and unemployment forced many islanders to emigrate to the Americas, mainly Cuba and Venezuela.

It was only in the 1880s that things really began to get better, largely due to Fernando León y Castillo, a local politician who became foreign minister in the Spanish government. With the collaboration of his brother, Juan, an engineer, he embarked on a project to transform Las Palmas into the major port on the island. Within about six years, the Puerto de la Luz was dealing with most of the steamship trade that passed through the islands.

WAR AND RECOVERY

The last of the briefly successful monocultures was bananas, introduced by the British in the late 19th century. But World War I had a disastrous effect on the trade, creating more poverty and more emigration. Contact with the New World, where Cuba had won freedom from Spain in 1898, led to calls for Canarian independence, but most people simply wanted the division of the archipelago into two separate provinces. Formalisation of this came in 1927 but no new economic solutions had been found when the three-year Spanish Civil War began in 1936, initiated by Francisco Franco, military governor of the Canary Islands. He spent the last night before launching his coup in the Hotel Madrid in Las Palmas.

BRITISH INTERESTS

There is a street in Las Palmas called Alfredo Jones, another called Tomás Miller, and the science museum is the Museo Elder. They were named after three of the British businessmen who had the most influence on Las Palmas in the 19th and early 20th centuries. There was a fourth – James Swanton – who seems to have been overlooked when street names were given out. British influence on the island was far reaching. Swanton and his young cousin, Thomas Miller, ran an import-export business, started in the 1820s. It flourished at the height of the cochineal boom and when aniline dyes killed demand, Miller began importing coal from Cardiff. The Santa Catalina jetty in the new port was financed by a second generation of Millers and Swantons; major shipping lines with offices in the port were British owned – one was the Elder-Dempster Line, in whose premises the Museo Elder is housed; and the water, electricity and telephone services were all set up by Englishmen. Sir Alfred Jones never lived on the island, but he founded the Grand Canary Coaling Company and financed the construction of the Hotel Santa Catalina. These wealthy businessmen established the British Club (still in Calle León y Castillo) and founded the first golf club. They built houses in the leafy Ciudad Jardín (Garden City) in Las Palmas and on the hills outside, in Tafira and Santa Brígida, still regarded as desirable places to live. For several decades at least, Gran Canaria was an informal colony of the British Empire.

After the civil war and World War II, the Canaries, like the rest of Spain, suffered from isolation and economic hardship. Things improved a little in the 1950s, when Spain was once more recognised by the international community, but it was the advent of tourism in the following decade that really turned the tide. Franco remained

Franco and his men at a secret meeting in Tenerife just before his coup

in power until his death in 1975, when his authoritarian regime was replaced by democratic government. The new Spanish Constitution of 1978 created the Autonomous Region of the Canary Islands – now one of 17 such regions. The archipelago is not completely separate from Spain but the island government, the Cabildo Insular, does have a great deal of freedom.

The islands have enjoyed considerable commercial freedom and tax exemptions ever since the 19th century, but when Spain became a full member of the European Union, fiscal changes had to be introduced. In order to protect trade and industry the Puerto de la Luz and the industrial area round Arinaga were confirmed as a Free Trade Zone, governed by a local consortium.

The economy is not too unhealthy, but it needs some support. The agricultural sector finds it difficult to compete in the wider market. Until the end of 1995, Spain guaranteed a market for Gran Canaria's bananas but since then, despite EU subsidies, the industry has been uneconomical. Production costs are high and bananas need a lot of water – a scarce

Mass tourism changed the face of Gran Canaria

commodity. The island is a major producer of tomatoes for the European market, but countries with lower labour costs, such as Morocco, have been able to undercut the Canarian growers. The only real money-spinner is tourism.

TOURISM AND THE ENVIRONMENT

The creation of the resorts of San Agustín, Playa del Inglés and Maspalomas in the 1960s, catering to sun-seeking northern Europeans, changed the face of Gran Canaria. This, together with the opening of Gando international airport in 1974, made tourism the main industry. The economy benefited enormously, and islanders gained employment, for most of the year at least, but inevitably there were effects on the environment. Hotels, swimming pools and golf courses are problematic for an island with a water shortage. Heavy traffic took its toll on the roads. And the island's reputation as a holiday destination suffered, too, from the alcohol-fuelled antics of some tourists.

For ecological and economic reasons, the Cabildo Insular has made huge efforts to diversify the tourist industry and protect the environment. Many areas have been designated natural parks and nature reserves; in fact, over 66,000 hectares (154,000 acres), some 40 percent of the island, is protected to some degree. Active environmental protection groups exert a steadying influence.

WIND, WATER AND FIRE

Water on the island is not only in short supply but, until relatively recently, had been in the hands of private suppliers. This has always been a contentious issue, and in the south it has been taken out of private hands and is run by a franchise called Canaragua. Water shortages have been alleviated to some extent by desalination plants – there are two huge ones run by a private company, Acciona Agua. Wind power has been introduced to keep costs down, and the huge wind farm at Pozo Izquierdo on the gusty east coast is the foremost example of this.

In July 2007 the island suffered from its worst forest fires in over 50 years. Low humidity, high temperatures and strong winds contributed to the dev-astation that led to more than 5,000 people being evacuated from their homes and around 20,000 hectares (50,000 acres) of ground being burnt, particularly in the mountainous region around Mogán. Fortunately no lives were lost. Two years later another wild fire in the south of the island damaged some 25,000 hectares (62,000 acres) and

Water is a scarce resource that must be handled carefully

forced a mass evacuation, but the region recovered remarkably well.

A GENTLER IMAGE

Gran Canaria's tourist industry suffered less than that in the rest of Spain during the economic downturn of the early 21st century, and tourist numbers have actually risen dramatically in recent years. The industry has been given a new direction, with less emphasis on sun, sea, sand and more on other aspects of the island. EU funds have helped to promote the *turismo rural* initiative by creating country hotels and converting traditional buildings into holiday accommodation. The opening up of the *caminos reales* (royal paths) in the island's interior are part of the drive to attract walkers and people with a love of the countryside. There has also been a resurgence of interest in the pre-Hispanic past, and in rediscovering the island's cultural heritage. Many people claim to be directly descended from the Guanches. In Gáldar, one of the two ancient capitals, which calls itself the Ciudad de los Guanartemes (City of Rulers), most of the streets have indigenous names, and the state-of-the-art Cueva Pintada Archaeological Museum tells the ancient story. An increasing number of children are being given Guanche names, such as Tamara or Tenesor, and a favoured name for bars and restaurants is Tagoror, which means a place of assembly. Perhaps this is part of a move to establish a new sense of island identity, while still being very much a part of Europe.

More children are being given Guanche names

HISTORICAL LANDMARKS

c. **1st–2nd centuries BC** Guanche settlements in Canary Islands.

AD1477–83 Spanish force lands on the island and subdues Guanches.

1492 Columbus briefly stops at Las Palmas before sailing to America.

c. **1500** Sugar cane introduced and African slaves imported. From 1554, the sugar industry declines.

1700–1950 Poverty forces widespread emigration to Latin America.

1830 An economic boom follows the introduction of the cochineal beetle.

1852 Isabella II declares the Canary Islands a Free Trade Zone.

1890 The British introduce bananas as a monoculture.

1911 Self-administration council – Cabildo Insular – introduced.

1927 The Canary Islands are divided into two provinces. Las Palmas de Gran Canaria becomes capital of the eastern province.

1936 Franco, military governor of the Canary Islands, initiates the three-year Spanish Civil War.

1956 The first charter plane lands on Gran Canaria. Tourism rapidly develops into the most important industry.

1974 Gando international airport opens.

1978–82 New Spanish Constitution joins the two island provinces to form the Autonomous Region of the Canary Islands.

1986 Spain joins the European Union and negotiates a special status for the Canary Islands.

1995 Islands integrated into the EU but retain important tax privileges.

2002 The euro becomes the national currency.

2005 Islands hit by Tropical Storm Delta, causing the destruction of the famous rock structure Dedo de Dios at Puerto de las Nieves.

2007 & 2009 Summer fires devastate the Mogán region.

2010–11 Gran Canaria (and Tenerife) buck the trend by attracting greater numbers of tourists despite the economic downturn.

2014 A record 3.13 million foreign tourists visit Gran Canaria. Oil spills affect beaches in the southern part of the island.

2015 A coalition between the Canarian Coalition and the Canarian Nationalist Party wins the Canarian parliamentary election.

WHERE TO GO

Gran Canaria is not a large island, but if you travel the short distance from the capital, Las Palmas, to the dunes of Maspalomas in the south, explore the lush Barranco de Agaete in the northwest, scale the mountainous central heights, or spend a peaceful day in one of the pretty fishing ports, you will feel that you have visited a small continent.

LAS PALMAS

Las Palmas ❶, capital of Gran Canaria, is a sprawling city with a population of over 382,000 people, nearly 80 percent of whom make their living in the service industries. There are several distinct focal points. To the south is the historical centre, Vegueta, a Unesco World Heritage Site since 1990. A busy dual carriageway divides Vegueta from the attractive old shopping district of Triana, with its cafés and Art Nouveau buildings. The traffic-filled Avenida Marítima and the noisy stretch of Calle León y Castillo lead to the next points of interest: lush Parque Doramas and the Muelle Deportivo, the yacht harbour. A further busy stretch, either following the sea or on a parallel road inland, leads to the huge Puerto de la Luz and lively Parque Santa Catalina. From here, a grid of streets links the city and the beach, Playa de las Canteras, which made Las Palmas a holiday resort before those in the south existed.

Between these points are the busy commercial streets around Avenida Mesa y López, the select Ciudad Jardín, where flowers blossom in walled gardens and government buildings fly their flags. At the far northern tip is La Isleta, a working-class district with some excellent fish restaurants; up on the hills behind is the Ciudad Alta where many

The spectacular dunes at Maspalomas

The Art Nouveau kiosk in Parque San Telmo

of the capital's citizens live and work.

TRIANA

Whether you come straight from the airport or on a bus trip from the south, you are likely to arrive at **Parque San Telmo Ⓐ**, for this is the site of one of the city's two bus terminals and the place where taxis wait to deliver passengers to other parts of town. There's a children's playground in the square and a pretty little chapel, the Ermita de San Telmo, whitewashed and simple outside, ornate and gilded within. Opposite, an Art Nouveau kiosk, decorated with gleaming tiles, serves drinks at tables under towering *fisco* trees; and the Quiosco de la Música stages concerts on Friday evenings. At the back of the square, a plaque on a military building informs that here, on 18 July 1936, Franco announced the coup that initiated the Spanish Civil War.

To the left of the square, the pedestrianised **Calle Mayor de Triana** has several attractive facades – some colonial in style, some Art Nouveau – and a medley of shops, ranging from a tiny fabric store and old-fashioned tobacconists, to branches of Zara and Marks & Spencer. To the right, in narrow, pretty streets reminiscent of the Triana district in Seville from which this area took its name, are smart boutiques and a few antiques and gift shops. The Librería del Cabildo Insular (www.libreriadelcabildo.com) on the corner of Cano and Travieso, has a wide choice of books and maps on the islands.

Calle Cano is also the place to find the **Casa-Museo Pérez Galdós B** (www.casamuseoperezgaldos.com; Tue–Sun 10am–6pm; guided tours on the hour). The building where the novelist was born in 1843 (see box) is a splendid example of Canary Island architecture, built around a courtyard and furnished with portraits and items from his houses in Madrid and Santander, many of which he designed and made himself. Further south on Calle Alfonso XIII is the beautiful blue building of the **Casa Africa**, (exhibitions Mon–Fri 10am–6.30pm; www.casafrica.es), which promotes African culture and celebrates relations between Europe, Africa and South America.

Close by is a little jewel of a square, the **Plazoleta de Cairasco.** The Hotel Madrid, one of the oldest in the city, serves meals and drinks at tables out under the palms till late at night. At the north end, the splendid **Gabinete Literario,** floodlit after dark, is an Art Nouveau treasure designated a 'Monumento Histórico Artistico'. Once a theatre, it is now home to a

FAMOUS SON

Benito Pérez Galdós (1843–1920) is widely regarded as one of the greatest Spanish novelists and playwrights, and many believe he would have received the Nobel Prize for Literature had it not been for his unpopular political views. His books and plays offer an inside view of Spanish life, and he was unusual in that he did not restrict himself to the world of just one social class. Born in Las Palmas, he spent much of his life in Madrid and Santander, where he became increasingly involved with politics. A staunch republican, he was elected as a senator for Madrid in 1910, and for Las Palmas when he returned in 1914. His greatest play, *Electra*, received its premier in the theatre named after him in Triana (www.teatroperezgaldos.es).

literary society (www.gabineteliterario.com), and also houses a restaurant/café with comfortable chairs on a shady terrace.

To the side of the little plaza runs the **Alameda de Colón**, at the north end of which, near a bust of Columbus, is the white-washed, colonial-style **Iglesia de San Francisco**. Destroyed in the fire of 1599, following Pieter van de Does' attack, it was rebuilt during the 17th century, then became a parochial church after the monks were ejected (as they were through-out Spain in 1821). At the south end of the *alameda* (tree-lined avenue), in an imposing building with stone-framed doorways, is a cultural centre, known by the acronym **CICCA**, where La Caja de las Canarias, a munificent savings bank, funds exhibitions, films, music and theatrical performances.

You are close now to the major highway (Calle Juan de Quesada) that separates Triana from Vegueta, but before you cross there's another attractive square. It is officially called

Twin-towered Catedral de Santa Ana

Hurtado de Mendoza, after an early 20th-century painter, but usually known as **Las Ranas** (The Frogs) because the long pool that runs down the centre is fed by two spouting frogs. A nearby café of the same name, in the Monopol Commercial Centre and opposite an imposing library building, is always buzzing with students at night. The university is a short distance up the highway, and there is some student accommodation in Triana. The Commercial Centre, in what used to be the grand Hotel Monopol, houses shops, bars, fast-food outlets, restaurants and a cinema.

VEGUETA

The historic centre of Las Palmas has a character all of its own. This was once the aristocratic quarter and its cobbled streets are lined with splendid colonial buildings with intricately carved balconies and intriguing, palm-filled courtyards, glimpsed when their huge, polished doors are ajar.

At its heart, in **Plaza de Santa Ana G**, is the twin-towered **Catedral de Santa Ana** (Mon–Fri 10am–4.30pm, Sat 10am–1.30pm; access only through Diocesan Museum). Started in 1497, it wasn't completed until the 20th century and is a mixture of architectural styles – Gothic, Renaissance and neoclassical. Elements on the facade and many of the statues inside are the work of the Canary Island sculptor, José Luján Pérez (1756–1815).

The adjoining **Museo Diocesano de Arte Sacro** (hours as above; entrance in Calle Espíritu Santo; www.diocesisde canarias.es) has a lovely cloister, the Patio de los Naranjos (Orange Trees). Among the sacred paintings and artefacts is an impressive modern series, *Stations of the Cross*, by local artist Jesús Arencibia. If you don't want to visit the museum and cathedral, you could take the modern lift (same hours; separate charge), which will whisk you to the top of one of the towers for a great view over the city.

The Casa de Colón is one of the city's most splendid buildings

Among the magnificent buildings in the plaza, the **Palacio Regental** may be the star. It is largely 17th century, although the facade dates from 1867. The Canarian balcony is older, as is the huge and splendid doorway, above which is the coat of arms of the kingdoms of León and Castile. Little remains of the adjoining **Palacio Episcopal** (Bishop's Palace) except an ornate single-storey facade. It was a victim of the fire of 1599, when Dutch privateer Pieter van der Does destroyed most of the town (see page 18).

Huge bronze dogs, the island's heraldic animal, sit outside the cathedral, and at the other end of the palm-lined square is the recently renovated, elegant 19th-century building housing the **Casas Consistoriales** (Offices of Island Government).

Beyond the square is the little Plaza Espíritu Santo with its unusual domed fountain in the centre. From here, Calle Dr Chil leads to the Museo Canario. This is a street of splendid houses with carved wooden balconies and intriguing, shady courtyards, most of which are now the homes and offices of lawyers.

The Vegueta food market on Calle Medizábel (Mon–Sat 6.30am–2pm) sells fruit and vegetables as well as fresh fish, local cured meats and cheeses. There are good local tascas and bars in the surrounding streets.

THREE VEGUETA MUSEUMS

The first of three Vegueta museums that deserve attention is the **Museo Canario** ⓓ (www.elmuseocanario.com; Mon–Fri 10am–8pm, Sat–Sun 10am–2pm) on Calle Dr Verneau. It houses the Canary Islands' largest collection of pre-Hispanic objects – pottery, tools, mummies and skeletons, and dozens of skulls, lined up in glass cases like macabre ornaments. Here you will see the ochre-coloured figure of the Idolo de Tara, a fertility goddess, copies of which are on sale in souvenir shops all over the island. There are also scale models of Guanche dwellings and a replica of the Cueva Pintada in Gáldar (see page 67). Further east, at Ramón y Cajal 1, in a beautifully refurbished 18th-century former hospital, is the San Martín Centro de la Cultura Contemporánea (www.sanmartincontemporaneo.com; Tue–Sat 10am–9pm, Sun 10am–2pm), a contemporary art gallery and concert hall.

The **Casa de Colón** ⓔ (www.casadecolon.com; Mon–Sat 10am–6pm, Sat 10am–3pm) is an endearing little museum, with ornate doorways and beautiful latticed balconies. Colón is the Spanish name for Columbus and it is claimed, with no supporting evidence, that he stayed here while one of his ships was being repaired. There is a replica of the cabin of *La Niña*, one of his fleet, nautical maps and charts, a collection of pre-Columbian artefacts from Ecuador and Mexico, and two

Columbus' prayer

A plaque on the wall of San Antonio Abad, the tiny chapel next to the Casa de Colón, claims that the explorer stopped to pray on this spot before setting off on his voyage of discovery.

noisy parrots which rule the inner courtyard. The house was the birthplace, in 1927, of the operatic tenor Alfredo Kraus.

The **Centro Atlántico de Arte Moderno** (CAAM; www.caam. net; Tue–Sat 10am–9pm, Sun 10am–2pm) is worth visiting mainly because it is a wonderful exhibition space – white walls, marble stairs and acres of glass, concealed behind a traditional facade. It has a good reputation as an educational and cultural centre, but visitors may find its changing exhibitions are generally of less interest than the building itself.

PARQUE DORAMAS AND THE PUEBLO CANARIO

Leave the old town now and get a bus (from Teatro Pérez Galdós on the Triana side of the highway, or from Parque San Telmo) to **Parque Doramas,** in a prosperous, leafy part of town known as the Ciudad Jardín. Amid tropical greenery in front of the ultra-smart **Hotel Santa Catalina**, a large statue dedicated to the vanquished chief Doramas shows aboriginal people leaping from a rocky fountain.

To the left of the hotel is the **Pueblo Canario** 🇫, a little complex of traditional island buildings with café tables in a central plaza. This Canarian village was designed in the 1930s by brothers Néstor and Miguel Fernández de la Torre, to interest early tourists in island ways. Costumed folk dancing displays are held here every Thursday at 5pm and Sunday at 11.30am (free). The **Museo Néstor** (www.museonestor alamo.com; Mon–Sat 10am– 3pm) dedicated to the better known of the brothers, is part

Leaping Guanches in the lush Parque Doramas

The 'Poema del Mar' exhibition room, Museo Néstor

of the complex. Born in Las Palmas, Néstor (1887–1938), always known simply by his first name, spent much of his life in Paris, Madrid and Barcelona, where he became famous for his sensuous paintings and imaginative stage designs. He returned to the island in later life with a heightened awareness of his roots and painted two series of works, *Atlantic Poem* and *Visiones de Gran Canaria* – both can be seen in the museum. There are also rooms dedicated to Canarian music and architecture.

Opposite the park is the Club Natación Metropol swimming and sports club (www.cnmetropole.com). Beside it, an underpass leads below the Avenida Marítima to the **Muelle Deportivo** Ⓖ, the yacht harbour, from where transatlantic yachtsmen set out, and visitors can take catamaran trips. The Match Cup Center includes a nautical bar, while the promenade beside the water is lined with restaurants, cafés and shops, making it a pleasant area, protected from the traffic on the road above. Adjoining the harbour area is the smart Real Club Náutico (www.rcngc.com) followed by the Playa de Alcaravaneras, a

Playing chess in Parque Santa Catalina

stretch of beach mostly frequented by local families, so busiest at weekends.

PARQUE SANTA CATALINA

If you want to do any shopping, head inland along broad Calle Mesa y López, where most of the big stores are found, including two branches of Spain's largest department store, El Corte Inglés. Otherwise, it's not far to the next point of interest, **Parque Santa Catalina** Ⓗ. Although dotted with palm trees and vivid flower beds, this, like San Telmo, is more of a square than a park, but much bigger and busier. There is always a sense of activity here, with visitors and local people frequenting the outdoor cafés; crowds of elderly men playing chess, dominos and cards under specially-erected awnings and lottery ticket vendors calling to attract attention. Here you can get local information from a small kiosk, board one of the open-topped, yellow *guagua turística* buses that allow you to hop on and off at sites of interest, or book tickets in the Fred Olsen office for the ferry to Tenerife. The company runs a free bus to Agaete to connect with the ferries.

AROUND THE PORT

On the port side of the park is the striking **Museo Elder** (www.museoelder.org; Tue–Sun 10am–8pm), a wonderful science and technology museum housed in a building that belonged to the Elder-Dempster Shipping Line, but has extended upwards and outwards. There are lots of interactive exhibits to amuse children, as well as an industrial robot spot-welding a car, a model of Foucault's pendulum, an incubator where patient visitors can watch chicks hatching from eggs, and an IMAX cinema.

A landscaped pedestrian area leads from the museum to the **Muelle Santa Catalina ❶**, in front of which an enormous, sail-like awning conceals a subterranean bus terminal. To the left of it, a shiny commercial centre in brilliant shades of blue and yellow, **El Muelle** (www.museoelder.org), overlooks the port. With numerous big-name stores, a cinema, disco, bowling alley and open-air restaurants and cafés, it has brought new life to this part of town.

PLAYA DE LAS CANTERAS

The stretch northwards from here along the huge **Puerto de la Luz** is all industrial buildings and traffic-clogged roads, so cross back to Parque Santa Catalina and make your way, via

The Museo Elder keeps visitors entertained for hours

Calle Luís Morote, through a maze of streets, where shops specialise in watches, cameras, mobile phones and all things electrical, and car-hire outlets, hotels and restaurants proliferate. Suddenly, you are on the other side of what has now become a narrow peninsula, and arrive at the beach.

Playa de las Canteras ❶ is the 3km (2-mile) stretch of sand that made the city Gran Canaria's very first tourist resort. It is lined with hotels and restaurants, some smart, some a little flaky, and some of which have been here since the 1960s heyday. A wide promenade runs the length of the beach; this busy walkway is dotted with palms, sun umbrellas that restaurants set out by the sea and the bright stalls of African traders selling clothing, carvings and jewellery.

These days the beach is more popular with visiting mainland Spaniards than with northern Europeans and they use it to the full, forming circles to play bingo and setting up tables

Playa de las Canteras is popular with locals and tourists alike

on which they lay out large picnic lunches. Ball games are forbidden during the day, but in the evening stretches of the beach become a football pitch. The natural reef, **La Barra**, a few hundred metres out, turns this stretch of coast into a natural lagoon, safe for children and non-swimmers.

BEACH EXTREMITIES

At the north end of the beach (where the peninsula is at its narrowest), old wooden fishing boats are pulled up on the sand. Follow the road behind La Puntilla, a windy point jutting out to sea, to reach the old fishermen's quarter of **La Isleta** Ⓚ. Here you can visit the sombre Castillo de la Luz, now used as an exhibition centre (hours vary depending on events) and, since 2015, the location of the **Fundación de Arte y Pensamiento Martín Chirino** (www.fundacionmartinchirino.org), which showcases the sculptures of local artist Martín Chirino. The main reason to come here is to scale the highest peak at **Las Coloradas** for a sweeping view of the sea, the mountains and the city – and to eat in El Padrino (see page 106). It's a long, steep climb, though, and you would do better to take a taxi or the No. 41 bus from Parque Santa Catalina.

At the southern end of Playa de las Canteras, beyond the reef's protective arm, constant on-shore winds make ideal conditions for surfers. This once-neglected area has been smartened up, with a promenade leading to the **Auditorio Alfredo Kraus**, home to the Las Palmas Philharmonic Orchestra. A large bronze statue of the tenor, who was born in the city, stands proudly outside. From a distance, the sand-coloured building appears to rise from the sea, and in some lights blends into the hills behind. Adjoining it is the Palacio de Congresos conference centre and, across the road, the huge **Las Arenas** commercial centre. From here, the arched bridge on the motorway heading northwest looks close enough to touch.

THE EAST

The lushest and loveliest part of Gran Canaria is the eastern region. It encompasses the verdant Barranco de Guayadeque, where there is still a small community of people living in caves, and several towns with delightful, well-preserved historic centres. It also includes the area south of Arinaga, where strong winds power Pozo Izquierdo, Gran Canaria's biggest wind farm. Those same winds help competitors during the world championship windsurfing competitions held at the Pozo Izquierdo Windsurf Center (tel: 928 121 400; www.pozo-ciw.com), which also offers windsurfing and other water sports to tourists.

Driving down the GC-1 motorway from the airport or from Las Palmas, you will not be aware of the treasures that lie only a few kilometres inland. Faceless as most motorways, it is lined with factories, out-of-town megastores and an airforce base, all set in a bare, scrubby landscape. It is, of course, the fastest way to reach the areas of interest, but if you are not in a hurry, you could explore the area on minor roads.

JARDÍN CANARIO

If you take the Santa Brígida road (GC-110) to the southwest of Las Palmas you can include the **Jardín Canario Viera y Clavijo ②** (www.jardincanario.org; daily 9am–6pm; free) on your itinerary. If you just want to make an excursion from Las Palmas to the garden you can take bus Nos 301 or 303 (in the direction of San Mateo). They leave every 15 minutes from the Parque San Telmo and the journey takes about 20 minutes. The botanical garden lies close to

Bus tips

If you visit the Jardín Canario by bus, ask the driver to tell you when you get there, or else he may not stop. Be prepared to cross the dual carriageway by an elevated pedestrian bridge to catch the bus back into town.

Discover local flora at Jardín Canario

the suburb of Tafira Alta, where elegant, early 20th-century villas and beautiful gardens are only slightly marred by the never-ending flow of traffic. The Jardín Canario is delightful, although the stepped, cobbled paths may rule it out for those who have difficulty getting around; some may wish that more of the fascinating specimens were identified.

The garden was established in 1952 by the Swedish botanist Eric R. Sventenius and is laid out along the steeply sloping side of a gorge. This can be crossed at one point by a wooden bridge to reach a flatter section where a cactus garden features an amazing selection of specimens from all over the world, many introduced to the island from the Americas in the 17th century. Just past the main entrance there are specimens of *Laurisilva* (bay laurel), which covered much of the island before the Spanish conquest but has long since been destroyed. There is also an avenue of dragon trees *(Dracaena draco)*, which were once believed to have healing properties, and a grove of *Pinus canariensis*, the indigenous pine tree. Allow a good couple of hours to visit the garden, because it is quite extensive and there is so much to see. Just outside the main entrance gate is a restaurant (www.restaurantejardincanario.com), which has a good reputation for serving typical Canarian food.

CALDERA DE BANDAMA

Just past Tafira Alta and Monte Lentiscal (the two prosperous suburbs virtually run into each other) drivers can take a left turn to the **Caldera de Bandama**. The volcanic crater is 1km (0.5 mile) wide and 200m (655ft) deep, and the best view of it is from the volcanic peak next door, the Pico de Bandama (574m/ 1,883ft), which has an observation platform and small bar – and you can drive to it. From here you also get magnificent views of the entire north and east coasts of the island. On a clear day you can sometimes see the neighbouring island of Fuerteventura to the northeast, while to the west looms the central massif.

Adventurous visitors can climb down into the crater itself, via a steep path that is visible from the rim – it takes about 30 minutes. At the bottom is an abandoned farmhouse, shaded by two enormous eucalyptus trees, and the outlines of terraced fields where vines were once cultivated.

South of the caldera, which is the Spanish word for cauldron but has become the international geological term for a volcanic crater, lies the largest golf course on the island – and the oldest one in Spain – the Real Club de Golf de Las Palmas. The club was founded at the end of the 19th century by some of the English expatriates who were so influential in the growth and prosperity of the city, and who were eager to indulge in one of their favourite forms of recreation.

TELDE

Back on the main road, turn left at San José on the cg-80 to **Telde ❸**. Follow signs to San Juan or the Centro Histórico and park as soon as you can, because Telde, the second-largest town on the island, is bedevilled by narrow, one-way streets and far too much traffic. There is a large modern section that is of little interest to visitors, but the old town, a protected conservation area since 1981, is well worth a stop. It centres on the attractive Plaza de San Juan, shaded by mature trees and surrounded by colonial-style houses with beautiful mosaic tiles and intricately carved balconies. Lording it over the square is the **Iglesia de San Juan Bautista** (daily from 10.30am but only if a custodian is available). Building began in 1519, but the neo-Gothic towers are early 20th-century additions. It houses a beautiful 16th-century Flemish altarpiece showing six scenes from the life of the Virgin, acquired when the town grew rich from the sugar trade. It is because the altarpiece is so valuable that the church is usually only open during services or when a guardian is available. The church's

Colourful facades in Telde

other treasure is an image of Christ made in Mexico from corn cobs. Just off the square is a children's park, with brightly-coloured birds in an aviary.

The street that links San Juan with the other historic district, San Fernando, is named, like many others in Gran Canaria, after Fernando and Juan León y Castillo, the brothers who transformed the port of Las Palmas. They were born in Telde and their home is now the **Casa-Museo León y Castillo** (www.fernandoleonycastillo.com; Tue–Sun 10am–6pm). It contains Spanish paintings from the 16th–20th centuries, along with sculpture and porcelain as well as a library.

CUATRO PUERTAS

Telde was one of the two Guanche capitals before the Spanish arrived (Gáldar was the other) and the indigenous people have left us an interesting archaeological site, just off the GC-100 from Telde to Ingenio. **Cuatro Puertas** (always open; free; free guided visits can be arranged by contacting Cabildo de Gran Canaria tel: 928 219 229), also known as Montaña Bermeja after the colour of its dark reddish stone, consists of a main chamber with four huge entrances. A shallow, semicircular enclave in the rock is thought to have been a sacrificial site, and the open space in front of the chamber was a tagoror, a place of assembly.

Recalling Ingenio's past

INGENIO

About 5km (3 miles) along the GC-100 lies the little town of **Ingenio** ❹. As you approach you will see the **Museo de Piedras y Artesanía** (Museum of Stones and Handicrafts; tel: 928 781 124; Mon–Sat 8am–6.30pm). It's an attractive building and there are some pieces of agricultural machinery on show and a few glass cases displaying minerals, but it is really a shop selling embroidered linen, pottery and ornaments.

A good road through the Barranco de Guayadeque

Ingenio is an attractive place famous for its delicacies such as pan de puño (fist bread), sold all over the island, and sopa de la Virgen (Virgin's soup). It was a prosperous sugar-refining centre in the 16th century (a model sugar press stands at the eastern approach to the town), but agriculture, chiefly tomato-growing, is the mainstay these days. Narrow alleys of whitewashed houses lead to the tiled **Plaza de la Candelaria**, where modern fountains contrast with a white, colonial-style church and the ochre-coloured town hall. Beside the church, bronze statues of women washing clothes add interest to another fountain.

BARRANCO DE GUAYADEQUE

Just before you reach the next town, Agüimes, 2km (1 mile) away, you will see a sign to the **Museo de Guayadeque** and **Centro de Interpretación Arqueológica** (Tue–Sat 9am–5pm, Sun 10am–3pm). This is the best route to take to the **Barranco de Guayadeque ⑤**, well-surfaced and less tortuous than the one from Ingenio, which also leads to the museum. The *barranco* is one of the most beautiful valleys on the island. Its steep slopes are honeycombed with cave dwellings (see box), and lush flora still thrives – cacti, tajinaste, palms and poppies, among other plantlife. The *barranco* is also home to one of the biggest lizards in the world – the *Lagarto canarión*; sparrow hawks can be seen in the skies and the sound of woodpeckers is loud in the pine woods higher up. There are still several functioning wells in the gorge; the Morro Verano, at 170m/555ft, is the deepest.

The *barranco* is for serious walkers, and there is a reliable organisation in Agüimes that arranges hikes if you want to go with a group (see page 88). If you go alone, make sure you

CAVE DWELLERS

The Centro de Interpretación is a helpful introduction to the life of the valley and its people, and displays some of the items – pottery, bones and textiles – that have been recovered from caves. More items are on display in the Museo Canario in Las Palmas. The *barranco* was the most densely populated gorge on the island during Guanche times. Early inhabitants farmed the slopes and even went down to the coast to fish, as the remains of sea-snail and limpet shells indicate. Numerous grain stores have been excavated and many mummified bodies were found in caves when interest in the area was stimulated at the end of the 19th century. The cave villages that exist today are rapidly being depleted. In 1970, there were some 450 inhabitants, now there are only about 90 people. There are still two chapels, and a functioning school, although it has fewer than a dozen pupils. Some crops are still grown – potatoes and corn in the higher regions, almonds on the lower slopes and on the valley floor – and some goats, pigs and sheep are kept, but most people now work in bars and restaurants, catering to the tourists.

have warm clothes for the chilly heights, strong shoes and plenty of water. However, there is much that can be enjoyed without doing anything too strenuous. The surfaced road continues for 9km (5 miles) or so beyond the Interpretation Centre, passing glorious scenery and reaching two cave villages, both still viable communities, with tiny chapels, a bar and rudimentary restaurant, and houses bright with geraniums. The road ends at the best-known cave restaurant, the Tagoror.

Small underground chapel in the Barranco de Guayadeque

AGÜIMES

Agüimes ❻ is one of the most appealing towns on the island. It's a place where the Ayuntamiento (Town Hall) takes seriously the job of preserving and improving the environment, and fostering conservation-conscious tourism – and it shows. The outskirts of the town, where there is a bus station and a public swimming pool, is pleasant enough, but the **Casco Histórico** is the place to go.

Spotless, narrow streets of ochre- and terracotta-coloured houses – several of them converted into *casa rural* accommodation – lead to the shady main square, **Plaza de Nuestra Señora del Rosario**, where there are a number of bars and cafés. Here, and in other parts of town, a number of bronze statues have been erected, portraying rural life and local characters. The neoclassical **Iglesia de San Sebastián**

Bronze statues, including this camel, are a feature of Agüimes

(daylight hours) at one end of the square, is a designated Monumento Histórico Artístico and has works by island sculptor José Luján Pérez. The Museo de Historia de Agüimes (Tue–Sun 9am–5pm) at calle Juan Alvarado y Saz 42 is also worth a visit if you're interested in local history. The tourist office, on Plaza San Antón, has an information centre with old photos and historical pieces. Soft classical music spills out from hidden speakers around a bronze statue of a female cellist, and a pretty café offers coffee and cake.

ARINAGA

For a real contrast, make the short trip from Agüimes to sleepy little **Arinaga**. As you will realise, this is a windy stretch of coast, but one much in favour with windsurfers. There is also a marine reserve and diving centre, at **Playa del Cabrón**. What is most immediately obvious, south of Arinaga, are the huge, graceful and surprisingly quiet wind turbines producing energy at the Pozo Izquierdo plant. Pozo Izquierdo beach is the site of events in the PWA World Cup Championships.

THE SOUTHERN RESORTS

The southern resorts of Gran Canaria are synonymous with package holidays, where sun, sea and sand keep visitors happy by day, and discos and bars ensure the alcohol is flowing and the music thumping until the early hours of the morning. The resorts of San Agustín, Playa del Inglés and Maspalomas, mini-cities built to provide instant gratification, were created out of this desert-by-the-sea (see box) and therefore have no history, no corners where remnants of an earlier way of life linger on. What they do have is year-round, reliably good weather, miles of rolling sands, water sports facilities, hotels and apartments with lush gardens and landscaped swimming pools; and restaurants, clubs, bars and shops by the score.

To the west of the three main resorts lie Puerto Rico and Puerto de Mogán. The former is also an artificial creation, but smaller and more low-key than its neighbours, and with an emphasis on family entertainment and water sports of all kinds. The latter was a struggling little fishing village until

The beach at Playa del Inglés, one of the tourist hotspots

the tourist boom began and has since been transformed into a delightful little resort built around a series of canals, with a wonderful sheltered harbour for yachtsmen.

SAN AGUSTÍN

Whether you are coming direct from the airport, from Las Palmas, or from Agüimes, you will approach the resorts on the GC-1 motorway. The first one, **San Agustín ➐**, was also the first to be built, in 1962. There is a plethora of hotels and apartment blocks, some cut off from the beach by the main road, over which there is a pedestrian bridge. The resort is growing, but it is still the smallest and quietest of the big three and caters mainly for retired couples and families with

THE COUNT'S VISION

The Conde del Castillo de la Vega Grande de Guadelupe, an aristocrat with a pedigree as long as his name, had a family home in Telde, in a building that is now the town hall. He also had large tracts of unused and seemingly useless land in the barren south of the island. Nobody lived there, nothing would grow there and the land was a liability. In the early 1960s, however, as the tourist boom swept through mainland Spain, the count came up with a scheme that would change the face and the economy of Gran Canaria. Out of the desert he constructed what are now the resorts of San Agustín, Playa del Inglés and Maspalomas. Tour companies, quick to spot a potential gold mine, soon moved building contractors in. Where else would you find streets named after tour operators as you do in Maspalomas? Within two decades the south of Gran Canaria had developed into a huge holiday complex, attracting visitors from northern Europe, mainly on all-inclusive package holidays, providing employment for islanders and further enriching the man who masterminded the project.

young children, although it is also very popular with wind-surfers (the F2 Surfcenter Dunkerbeck school is here). There is a fairly small, safe beach, a variety of water sports facilities and some attractive apartments, most set in gardens among palms and poinsettia, and with their own pools.

The Playa del Inglés promenade at dusk

Following the paved promenade to the west of the resort you reach **Playa de las Burras**, known as Playa Chica – the little beach – around which cluster a villa complex, a well-stocked supermarket, a small shopping centre and a number of modern apartment blocks and hotels.

PLAYA DEL INGLÉS

You can walk along the promenade from San Agustín to **Playa del Inglés ❽**. As you go, you will notice that the sand becomes more golden, the apartment blocks get taller and visitors' clothing grows scantier. Approach direct from the motorway and you will find yourself suddenly in a grid of wide streets lined with large hotels, restaurants, car-hire outlets and retail opportunities, and peopled by a relentless march of tourists carrying beach gear.

Playa del Inglés is a big place, but there is a good bus service, taxis are cheap and reliable, and hotels further from the beach provide frequent free buses. There are several huge commercial centres, the largest being the oddly-named

The dunes of Maspalomas offer a wonderful sense of freedom

Yumbo Centre, in which you will find the main tourist information office (see page 130), presided over by efficient, multilingual staff. Among the numerous bars and clubs in the centre are quite a few that cater to the gay community.

The beach is the main event, of course. The **Paseo Costa Canaria** is an attractive pedestrian promenade, lined with villa complexes and bright with tropical blooms, that runs the length of it, from Playa de las Burras to the point where the Maspalomas dunes begin. On the sands below, sun loungers and beach umbrellas are arranged in serried ranks, and the more energetic visitors try their hand at water-skiing, windsurfing and parasailing.

Descend via stairs or escalators to the **Paseo Marítimo**. Protected by awnings from the heat of the sun, this is a 2km (1.25-mile) stretch of fast food outlets, amusement arcades, Irish pubs and German beer kellers with extended happy hours, tattoo parlours, internet cafés and shops selling beachwear.

MASPALOMAS

Maspalomas ❾ is divided from Playa del Inglés by a spectacular stretch of **dunes**, covering an area of 4 sq km (1.5 sq miles), that in 1994 were designated a nature reserve in order to preserve the ecosystem. The contrast between these pristine mountains of sand and the commercialism of the resort is quite remarkable. You can walk over the dunes if you protect your feet from the hot sand, but it is hard going and takes over an hour. Following the beach around takes half the time, and you will pass a popular nudist stretch en route. Adjoining the dunes, a golf course forms another barrier between the neighbourhoods, but inland the two resorts almost merge into each other, although their style is distinctive. Accommodation in Maspalomas is in smart hotels, bungalows or low-rise apartment complexes in large, lush gardens, for this is altogether a more upmarket resort.

The main road swoops past **Aqualand** waterpark (daily 10am–5pm; www.aqualand.es) and the huge **Holiday World** amusement park (www.holidayworld-maspalomas.com; daily 6–11pm), all the way round the sprawling Maspalomas development to **El Faro**, the lighthouse. From here a palm-lined *paseo* leads to the area known as **El Oasis**, with some smart hotels and other more affordable apartments, beside **La Charca** (see box). You can drive back up Avenida Oceania, which parallels a palm-fringed dry river bed that runs straight through the middle of the *urbanización*.

La Charca

La Charca, part of the Maspalomas nature reserve, is a little lagoon to which migratory and breeding birds, frightened away by human activity, are being encouraged to return. Moorhens, herons and kestrels have ventured back to its reed beds and ospreys have occasionally been seen.

To the west of the lighthouse, in a sheltered bay, lies the luxury resort of **Hotel Riu Palace Las Meloneras**, with everything for the discerning visitor, while further inland **Sonnenland** is a low-key, family-oriented tourist complex.

INLAND EXCURSIONS

When the swimming pool loses its sparkle and the beach becomes a bore, there are plenty of excursions available just a little way inland. A car isn't necessary because there are regular bus services from convenient stops in all the resorts. **Mundo Aborigen** (www.mundoaborigen.com; daily 9am–6pm), a well-structured re-creation of life in a Guanche settlement, and the **Camel Safari Park La Baranda** (www.camelsafarigrancanaria.com; Mon–Sat 8am–6pm) are both a few kilometres up the road to Fataga, while **Palmitos Park** (www.palmitospark.es; daily 10am–5pm), a big ornithological park with an aquarium, butterfly house and botanic garden is on the road inland from Maspalomas. **Sioux City** (http://siouxcitypark.es; Tue–Sun 10am–5pm), a Wild West theme park, lies in the Cañon del Águila, just east of San Agustín.

Playa de Amadores near Puerto Rico

PUERTO RICO

The GC-1 motorway continues along the coast to Puerto Rico. The first community west of Maspalomas (on the old coast road) is **Pasito Blanco**, a little port and resort mainly of interest to sailing enthusiasts. Next comes **Arguineguín**, which

Puerto Rico and its "giant amphitheatre" of apartment blocks

has seen quite a bit of development in recent years, but is still a working fishing port and community and rather pleasant after so much artificiality. Elderly men playing draughts in the Centro Socio Cultural don't seem bothered by the comings and goings of the tourists who disembark from cruise ships or pleasure craft, mostly bound for the larger resorts nearby.

If you want to expand and develop a pleasant little bay surrounded by sheer cliffs, you can build a landscaped promenade and a few attractive seaside villas, but after that the only way to go is up. That is what the entrepreneurs of **Puerto Rico** ❿ did when the resort was conceived in the 1970s and the result is a wall of apartment blocks rising to the top of the hills, like tiers of seats in a giant amphitheatre. Below, space is at a premium, and sun beds are even lined up along the length of the jetty. The clean little beach is family-oriented – the families are predominantly English – and children will love the huge water slide at **Atlantida**

water park (daily 10am–5pm). There are also several large, modern commercial centres.

Puerto Rico has a serious reputation as a sailing centre and members of its club have won five Olympic medals. Deep-sea fishermen, not to be outdone, have claimed nearly three dozen world records in their sport. Naturally, the **Puerto Deportivo** caters for visiting fishing and water sports enthusiasts. There are diving schools and sailing schools, deep-sea fishing trips, 'dolphin search' trips in glass-bottomed catamarans, or simple pleasure trips that run up and down the coast.

PUERTO DE MOGÁN

Built round a complex of sea-water canals with delicately arched bridges, **Puerto de Mogán** ⓫ is almost impossibly pretty. The windows and flat roofs of its two-storey houses are outlined in shades of blue, green and ochre, the walls smothered with multicoloured bougainvillaea and trailing geraniums.

There are two ports here: the working one that was once the town's *raison d'être* and from which a fishing fleet still operates, and the **Puerto Deportivo**, where luxurious yachts bob in the water. This leisure port is lined with cafés and restaurants, all offering wonderful views and similar fish and seafood menus. The buildings that line the streets behind the harbour are equally picturesque and some of them house more restaurants and a few above-average gift

Fishing fiestas

The Fiestas del Carmen, celebrating the patron saint of fishermen, take place throughout July in Arguineguín and Puerto de Mogán. Celebrations include firework displays, concerts and dances and culminate in a maritime procession, led by a decorated boat carrying the statue of the Virgin.

Puerto de Mogán still has a fishing fleet

shops, but most are holiday apartments belonging to the Hotel Puerto de Mogán (see page 137).

Submarine Adventure offers trips in a yellow submarine and pleasure boats ply back and forth between here, Puerto Rico and Arguineguín, but most visitors are content simply to wander the streets and sit in the cafés, or make for the small, sheltered beach to the east of the port, which has been 'sandscaped' and extended.

On Friday a huge market lines the quay, selling African carvings, bead jewellery, aromatherapy oils, island cheeses, exotic fruits and beach sarongs. Busloads of tourists arrive from neighbouring resorts around 10.30am and are whisked away with their purchases in the afternoon.

MOGÁN

The road inland wends its way up the fertile, fruit-producing *barranco* to Mogán. In season, you may be able to buy ripe papaya, mangoes and avocados by the roadside. Just before the town, a windmill stands sentinel by the road in the tiny hamlet of El Molino de Viento – which means windmill. Surrounded by jagged mountains, **Mogán ⑫** is a sleepy little place with a picture-postcard church dedicated to San Antonio, colourful, well-watered gardens in the central plaza and towering palms outside the town hall. If you come in high season, when visitors drive up from the coast in hired jeeps, there will be a buzz of activity on the streets and in a couple of rather good restaurants. Otherwise, the sound of goats bleating in the *barranco* may be the only noise you hear.

GOING WEST

The west of Gran Canaria is for those who like a challenge. It is the area least visited by tourists; the roads are vertiginous and villages few and far between. But there

A sinuous road snakes through the bare hills

are stunning rock formations and mountain landscapes, marvellous views and a chance to experience a region that feels quite remote although it's only a few hours' drive from Las Palmas.

The beach at Güi-Güi

THE MOUNTAIN ROUTE

The road from Mogán (GC-200) twists and turns on its way to San Nicolás de Tolentino, cutting through rocks of red, grey and gold and passing isolated houses where convolvulus clings to crumbling walls. To your right soar the Montaña de Sándara, the Montaña de las Monjas, and the peak of Inagua, all over 1,400m (4,600ft) high. To the left, three deep gorges run down to the sea. The first is the **Barranco de Veneguera**, where a track – which should only be attempted in a four-wheel-drive vehicle – leads 10km (6 miles) through banana plantations to a lovely, unspoiled beach. The barranco is part of the Parque Rural del Nublo and cannot be developed for tourism.

The road running through the next gorge, the **Barranco de Tasarte**, is a bit better, and also culminates in a pretty beach. From the third gully, the **Barranco de Tasártico**, there is a long, arduous hike through the **Reserva Natural Especial de Güi-Güi**, where 3,000 hectares (7,400 acres) of land are protected to safeguard the vegetation clinging to the rocks. Those who can go the distance will be rewarded with an idyllic little beach. Just past the Tasarte turning, to the right of the road, is **La Fuente de los Azulejos**, where oxidisation has turned the rocks bright green. Opposite, a

You say tomato

The tomato industry is not as prosperous as it once was, as it now faces stiff competition from Moroccan growers. Despite this, the region still exports some 100,000kg (220,000lbs) of early varieties per annum. The *tomate aliñado* is a popular tapas dish: a huge local tomato comes sliced and dressed in olive oil, vinegar and lots of garlic.

roadside bar sells papaya juice to drink and aloe vera to ease sunburn.

SAN NICOLÁS DE TOLENTINO

As the road begins to straighten, you come to the village of **Tocodomán**, and **Cactualdea** (daily 10am–6pm). This 'Cactus Village' has more varieties of cacti than you knew existed, all well-labelled and set among palms and dragon trees. There is also a replica Guanche cave, a restaurant serving typical Canarian dishes, wine tasting opportunities and, of course, a gift shop.

You won't be able to miss the fact that swathes of land here are covered in plastic. Beneath the plastic grow tomatoes, the crop that is the mainstay of the region and of its only proper town, **San Nicolás de Tolentino** (officially known as La Aldea de San Nicolás). The town does not have a lot going for it, but it's a friendly place that tries hard to attract visitors. A tourist office on the right as you enter town offers informative leaflets and has *artesanía* items for sale, the woven textiles showing distinct Latin American influences. The town used to be a craft centre but these days weaving and pottery are hobbies rather than industries. There are a few small hotels and a couple of restaurants offering 'home-style cooking'.

PUERTO DE LA ALDEA

Some 3km (2 miles) down the road is **Puerto de la Aldea** ⑬ – which simply means Port of the Village. The port is tiny, but there seems to be enough fish brought in to keep several restaurants flourishing. Beside a pebbly beach is a smartly tiled promenade; parallel to it runs a shady garden with stone picnic tables set beneath pine trees. At the far end lies **El Charco** (The Lagoon), a fairly nondescript pond for most of the year but on 11 September the site of the Fiesta del Charco, when local people attempt to catch fish with their bare hands and to duck each other in the water. The origins of this strange custom are uncertain, but it is believed to date from pre-Hispanic times. *Lucha canaria* (wrestling) matches and *juego del palo* (stick-fighting) competitions are an integral part of the festival.

An aboriginal settlement close by, **Los Caserones**, has yielded a great many archaeological finds, including the bones of a Verdino dog, the emblem of the Canary Islands. The remains of the settlement can be seen on a small hill.

The stunning view from the Mirador del Balcón

THE COASTAL ROAD

The journey up the coast is one that demands concentration. The road winds past bare rock on one side and steep cliffs, plunging straight into the ocean, on the other. Fortunately, two *miradores* (viewpoints) have been created at points of particular beauty, so drivers can stop to admire the views. The first is the **Mirador del Balcón**, the second the **Andén Verde**. To the north the craggy coastline runs up to the Punto de Góngora; straight ahead, across miles of dark blue sea, lies Tenerife, crowned with the peak of El Teide, at 3,718m (11,898ft) the highest mountain in Spain.

PUERTO DE LAS NIEVES

You pass only one village along the way, El Risco, and there are still many curves to go before you arrive at **Puerto de las Nieves ⓮** (The Harbour of the Snows). The name derives not from any freak snowfall but from Nuestra Señora de las Nieves, the Madonna of the Snows, patron saint of the local fishermen. Her tiny chapel, known as the **Ermita de**

BRINGING DOWN THE BRANCHES

Puerto de las Nieves and Agaete are renowned for a festival known as Bajada de las Ramas (Bringing Down the Branches), celebrated with great enthusiasm on 4–5 August each year. Residents of the two communities gather branches from the hillsides and carry them down to the harbour, where they whip the waves with them before laying them at the feet of the Virgin of the Snows. Although this provides a religious context, the ritual has pagan origins, and, like many festivals, was intended to bring both rain and fertility. It's a high-spirited occasion, with lots of music and dancing, feasting and frolicking, and people come from all over the island to take part.

las Nieves (by appointment only outside Mass times), houses a real treasure, a 16th-century Flemish triptych attributed to Joos van Cleve, depicting the Virgin and Child flanked by saints Francis and Anthony. The decorated wooden ceiling above the choir is said to be Mudéjar, the architecture of the Moors who remained in Spain after the reconquest in the late 11th century.

In the harbour fishing boats bob gently beside a new jetty, where wooden decking has been laid down for the benefit of sunbathers who can't find a comfortable

Celebrating the patron saint of fishermen, Puerto de las Nieves

spot on the pebble beach. There is a sheltered bay which is good for swimming. A number of restaurants line the quay, serving excellent fish at reasonable prices. They get very busy at weekends, when people from Las Palmas come for lunch. Otherwise, the main bursts of activity are the arrivals and departures six times a day of the ferries to Santa Cruz de Tenerife, run by the Fred Olsen line (a free bus from Las Palmas connects with the port).

A great deal of investment has gone into the village in an attempt to compensate for the declining fishing industry. A large hotel has been built close to the remains of a Guanche cemetery, but on the whole the development has been sympathetic. A promenade, called the Paseo de los Poetas, has been constructed, and some low-rise apartment blocks and villas have sprung up in the streets behind it, blending quite nicely with the single-storey fishermen's cottages.

At the southern end of the village, at the foot of the dramatic coastline, the stump of the **Dedo de Dios** (Finger of God), rises from the sea. The 'finger' itself, once a famous local landmark, was destroyed by a storm in November 2005.

AGAETE

Return to the main road and almost immediately you are in **Agaete ⑮**, where a number of the houses have carved wooden balconies. In the Plaza de la Constitución, as you enter the town, stands the imposing, 19th-century Iglesia de la Concepción, and nearby, off Calle Huertas, the **Huerto de las Flores** (Tue–Fri 9am–5pm, Sat 9am–2.30pm; free) is a small botanical garden with some rare trees. On the outskirts

Barranco de Agaete

is the **Parque Arqueológico de Maipés** (www.arqueologia canaria.com; Tue–Sun 10am–2pm in winter, until 6pm in summer), a Guanche necropolis.

The town stands at the entrance to the **Barranco de Agaete**, a dramatic green and fertile gorge signposted simply as **El Valle** (The Valley). It's a lovely place to drive or walk. Avocados, oranges, lemons and mangoes grow on terraces clinging to the steep sides of the valley. Lofty Canary palms, solitary agaves and prickly pears gradually give way, on the upper slopes, to the Canary pine.

The road only goes as far as the little village of Los Berrazales, and down a dirt track just before you reach it stands the atmospheric Finca Las Longueras (www.laslongueras.com), a *hotel rural* housed in a 19th-century colonial mansion (see page 138).

THE NORTH

There are some 700 hectares (1,730 acres) of protected land in the north of the island, the best known area being the **Reserva Natural de los Tilos de Moya**. Away from these reserves, the landscape is fairly barren, for the forests of bay laurel (*Laurus canariensis*) that once covered it in green were cut down in the 16th century to provide fuel for the sugar industry. Yet more land was cleared to make way for bananas, introduced as a monocrop by the English more than three centuries later. The principal crop today is still bananas, many of which are grown in mammoth plastic tunnels.

In marked contrast to the sparsely populated west coast, this small area encompasses half a dozen towns: Gáldar, Guía, Moya, Arucas, Firgas and Teror. All are worth visiting and all involve circuitous, winding roads. It is often easier to return to the main coastal road between towns, rather than take what looks like the shortest route.

GÁLDAR

The hill on which **Gáldar** ⑯ is set resembles an extinct volcano, with the town clustered at its feet. It is only about 8km (5 miles) between Agaete and Gáldar, but the pace of life seems to shift up a notch. Park as soon as you find a space because traffic is heavy and the one-way streets are confusing.

Gáldar is known as the Ciudad de los Guanartemes (City of Rulers), as it was the seat of Tenesor Semidan, one of the island's two Guanche chiefs. The town is proud of its heritage and many of the streets and squares have Guanche names. Post-conquest Gáldar was founded in 1484 and was the capital of Gran Canaria before Las Palmas.

The Iglesia de Santiago de los Caballeros in Gáldar

The **Iglesia de Santiago de los Caballeros**, in a shady square, was built on the spot where Semidan's palace supposedly stood. Begun in 1778, it was the first neoclassical building on the island. It houses a number of statues attributed to José Luján Pérez (1756–1815), who was born nearby in Santa María de Guía. The Ayuntamiento (Town Hall), in the same square, has a huge dragon tree in its courtyard. Planted in 1718, it is said to be the oldest in the archipelago. At the side of the square you will find the tourist office and the Teatro Municipal.

The Patrimonio Histórico – the department in charge of cultural affairs – was somewhat slow to exploit Galdár's legacy, but the Museo y Parque Arqueológico Cueva Pintada (www.cuevapintada. com; Tue–Sat 10am–6pm, Sun 11am–6pm) is now open in Calle Audiencia, in the

Guanche sculptures

At the eastern entrance to Gáldar a sculpture represents three Guanche princesses. Another sculpture in the town depicts Tenesor Semidan, the chief who reluctantly accepted baptism and collaborated with the Spanish.

town centre, on the site of the Guanche Painted Cave. Visitor can buy tickets in advance on site and through the website (http://valora.entrees.es). Another important archaeological site, reached by a lane running through banana plantations towards the coast, is the **Poblado y Necrópolis de la Guancha**, consisting of the remains of circular tombs and a number of houses, where numerous mummies were found. The site is currently only open by prior arrangement (tel: 928 219 421 ext. 4441).

SARDINA

From the roundabout to the west of Gáldar (the same way you came in), the main road west leads to **Sardina**, a tiny resort on a small beach, popular with snorkellers and protected by dark, volcanic rocks. A harbour-side restaurant offers satisfying fish dishes and a view of the beach. Sardina is pretty quiet during the week but attracts people from Gáldar and Las Palmas at weekends. North of the village a lighthouse stands on the windy Punta de Sardina.

SANTA MARÍA DE GUÍA

The next town, going east from Gáldar at the same roundabout, is little **Santa María de Guía** ⑰, usually just known as

The pre-Hispanic Cenobio de Valerón is an intriguing place

Guía, famous for its award-winning *queso de flor*. This is a cheese made from sheep and cows' milk, mixed with the juice of cardoon thistle flowers. It sounds a little strange but tastes delicious. A traditional cheese festival is held here at the end of April and beginning of May and continues on nearby Montaña Alta.

There are some attractive, brightly painted houses in Guía's Casco Histórico, and an imposing, two-towered church in the Plaza Grande (not very big, despite its name) where a market is held every Tuesday morning.

CENOBIO DE VALERÓN

Take the main road now for Moya, but turn off first where you see signs to the **Cenobio de Valerón** ⓲ (www.arqueologiacanaria.com; winter 10am–5pm, summer 10am–5pm). *Cenobio* means convent and this complex of some 300 caves, hollowed out of the soft, volcanic rock, was once believed to have been a place where *harimagüadas* – young virgins

– were detained in order to protect their purity until they married. However, it is now widely accepted that the caves were grain stores, which were easily defensible because of their isolated position.

MOYA

The GC-75, the next turning off the main road, winds up hill to friendly, sleepy little **Moya** ⑲. There is a helpful tourist office and an impressive church, **Nuestra Señora de Candelaria**, begun in the 16th century but with many later additions. It is home to some interesting pieces of sculpture, including a 15th-century cedar wood figure of the Virgin of Candelaria, and several works by Luján Pérez, but unfortunately it is often closed except for early evening services.

Moya is the birthplace of the island's best-loved poet, Tomás Morales (1885–1921) and his home, the **Casa-Museo Morales** (www.tomasmorales.com; Tue–Sun 10am–6pm, until 7pm in summer) stands in the square opposite the church. It's an intimate little place with first editions of Morales' work, his Remington typewriter and lots of photos, paintings and poems.

A bronze statue of the poet stands outside. Morales is one of the poets after whom the Paseo de los Poetas in Puerto de las Nieves was named. The other two are his contemporaries, Alonso Quesada and Saulo Torón.

A portrait of Morales in the museum dedicated to him

From the top of the town a road leads past neatly cultivated vegetable gardens on the valley slopes to **Los Tilos**

de Moya, a 91-hectare (225-acre) nature reserve – although it is laurels not *tilos* (limes) that are being protected. Swathes of them once covered the island but few remain, and the protection order has been placed in an attempt to re-establish them.

ARUCAS

Unless you want to visit the centre of the island, retrace your route to the main coast road or motorway and at Bañaderos, take the turning to **Arucas** ⑳. As you enter the town, the **Parque Municipal** is on your left, a shady spot full of exotic trees and plants. You will soon get pulled into the busy one-way system, so park as soon as possible and explore the **Casco Histórico** on foot. The huge lava-stone church of **San Juan Bautista** (daily 9.30am–12.30pm, 4.30–7pm; free), begun in 1909, is said to owe its inspiration to Antoni Gaudí's Sagrada Família in Barcelona, and there are some similar

A lava-stone church dominates Arucas

Modernista flourishes. Inside, it is more conventionally neo-Gothic, and has three splendid rose windows.

In the nearby Calle León y Castillo a statue of the poet Domingo Rivero, book in hand, stands in front of a giant cactus outside the Casa de Cultura. Rivero, great-uncle of Tomás Morales, was born here in 1852. Inside, leading off a pleasant courtyard with a dragon tree, are much-frequented reading rooms for adults and children.

One of the reasons traffic is heavy in Arucas is that tourists' vehicles must wend their way through the old town to reach the nearby **Montaña de Arucas**. This is where the Guanche leader, Doramas, was killed in single-handed combat by Pedro de Vera in 1480. His followers are said to have leapt to their deaths in the *barranco* rather than surrender. Today, there's an observation point offering great views.

FIRGAS AND THE FINCA DE OSORIO

From Arucas there are two routes to Teror. The longer one, on the GC-300, will take you via the pleasant little town of **Firgas**, where a man-made waterfall cascades 30m (90ft) down shallow steps in the centre of a pedestrianised street. Firgas is known for its water. There's a natural spring just south of the town and the remarkably tasty product is bottled and sold all over the island.

The more direct route is on the GC-43. This one will take you past the **Finca de Osorio** (by prior appointment only at visitalafincadeosorio@gmail.com; daily 9am–5pm). This rural mansion is used as an *Aula de la Naturaleza* – a place where school groups and college students come, some on residential courses, to learn about conservation, wildlife and agriculture. The formal gardens are rich with roses and magnolias and the forested land around the house is a favourite picnic spot for local families.

TEROR

Teror ㉑ is a delightful little town with some of the best examples of colonial-style architecture you will find outside Las Palmas. Carved wooden balconies adorn sparkling white facades and huge doors open onto courtyards filled with ferns. It is also the home of Virgen del Pino (Madonna of the Pine Tree). In 1481, as the island was being subdued by the forces of Pedro de Vera, local shepherds are said to have had a vision of the Virgin appearing to them at the top of a pine tree. The miraculous apparition gave rise to a cult, and today the town has a number of lovely churches dedicated to the Virgin. In the centre stands the **Basilica de Nuestra Señora del Pino** (Mon 1–8pm, Tue–Fri 9am–1pm, 3–8pm, Sat 9am–8.30pm, Sun 7.30am–7.30pm; free), begun in 1767, where the richly clothed statue of the Virgin is displayed, surrounded by votive gifts and symbols. The Virgin del Pino is perhaps the best-loved saint on the island and pilgrims flock to Teror all year round, but especially on her feast day, 8 September. A huge festival is held during that week, with traditional music and dancing and plenty of cheerful secular celebrations accompanying sombre religious rituals.

Behind the church are stalls selling local produce – homemade bread, cheese and vegetables – as well as religious items. In front stands the Palacio Episcopal (Bishop's Palace), which now houses a cultural centre. On the right-hand side of the basilica, is the **Casa Museo de los Patronos de la Virgen del Pino** (tel: 928 630 239; Mon–Fri 11am–4pm, Sun 10am–2pm) in a beautiful building, set around

Virgin's gifts

A sensible sign in the Basilica de Nuestra Señora del Pino reads: 'Although the Virgin is grateful for your gifts and candles she would rather you gave your money to the poor.'

Historic, colonial-style buildings in Teror

a courtyard and furnished in the style of a noble, 17th-century home. It belongs, as it always has, to the Manrique de Lara family, who still spend the festival week here. At the back of the house are an old bakery and a stable block, where Don Manrique's polished 1951 Triumph shares space with sedan chairs, carts and carriages.

There is a smaller square close by, the **Plaza Teresa de Bolívar**, with a stone fountain in the centre. It is named after the first wife of Simón de Bolívar, the man who led the liberation of many of the Spanish colonies in South America in the 19th century. Her family came from Teror; his from Tenerife. The couple met in Venezuela, but Teresa died less than a year after they were married.

The centre of Teror is closed to traffic, so you can wander through the cobbled alleys and little squares and drink in the atmosphere without being disturbed by noise or fumes. If you come on Sunday morning you will also be able to enjoy the busy, and very local, market.

THE CENTRAL PEAKS

In order to appreciate the age and majesty of the planet and the relative insignificance of human beings, all you need is a trip to the central peaks of Gran Canaria. Over millions of years volcanic eruptions, fierce winds and driving rain have moulded and sculpted the rocks into strange shapes, and erosion has also created deep *barrancos* (gorges) that radiate out from the centre and descend to the coast, their fertile soil supporting lush vegetation.

The highest peaks are Pico de las Nieves (Peak of the Snows) at 1,949m (6,394ft), followed by Roque Nublo (Rock of Clouds), at 1,803m (5,915ft), and Roque Bentaiga (1,412m/4,632ft). Below them, mountain villages cling to the rock, and narrow terraces are cultivated wherever possible. Much of the central area is protected as part of the Parque Rural del Nublo; while the land to the west of

The mountainous interior is great hiking country

Artenara forms the Parque Natural de Tamadaba. While the mountains obviously have a huge appeal for climbers and serious walkers, there are many relatively short and easy walks that can be made amid stunning scenery, some of them on the *caminos reales* (see page 81), others on newer paths.

The central region can be reached quite easily from most parts of the island: direct from Las Palmas; from the northern towns of Arucas and Moya; from Agüimes in the east; or from the southern resorts, via the Barranco de Fataga. Only from the wild west coast, where tracks either peter out altogether or challenge the toughest vehicles and most confident drivers, are the peaks inaccessible.

If you're approaching from Las Palmas you can take the Santa Brígida road through **Vega de San Mateo** (usually known simply as San Mateo) and up the tortuous road to Tejeda, where bus drivers sound their horns as they approach every sharp bend. Or you could avoid the stress and take bus No. 303, changing in Vega de San Mateo. There is a small museum of rural life here (mornings only) and on Sunday, a large farmers' market. As the road climbs upwards, the lush vegetation changes. If you go in spring or early summer you will notice rampaging nasturtiums, blossoming lavender bushes and neat orange groves on the first part of the journey. Next come the prickly pear cactus *(Opuntia ficus indica)* eucalyptus trees and century plants *(Agave)*, before the entire hillside turns yellow with broom and, close to the top, the pines and holm oaks begin.

CRUZ DE TEJEDA

The top of the pass, at 1,580m (5,184ft), is marked by a sombre, stone crucifix, the **Cruz de Tejeda ㉒**. Surrounded by towering peaks, this is a hive of commercial activity, with two

The sombre stone cross at Cruz de Tejeda

bustling restaurants (one, El Refugio, is also a hotel), a shop specialising in aniseed-flavoured cakes, and a row of stalls selling embroidered tablecloths, ponchos, beach towels, dried fruit and stuffed camels. There is also a man offering donkey rides to children.

Behind the cross stands a hotel, the beautifully renovated four-star **Parador Hotel de Cruz de Tejeda** (see page 139), which was designed in the 1930s by Néstor Martín-Fernández de la Torre. Magnificent panoramic views can be enjoyed from the hotel, as well as spa and fitness facilities.

The view is dominated by the impressive, pointing finger of **Roque Nublo** ㉓, which will have been visible for some time. Depending on the weather and the time of day, the huge monolith appears to change colour and is not hard to understand why the Guanches revered this as a holy place. *A camino real* (see box) leads from Cruz de Tejeda to Roque Nublo, but there is a shorter walk from Ayacata. On a clear morning, especially, there is a breathtaking view across the entire island. Away in the distance, Tenerife's Mt Teide, snow-capped for much of the year, seems to rise straight out of the sea.

ARTENARA

It is a difficult but beautiful drive from Tejeda to **Artenara** ㉔, which, at an altitude of 1,270m (4,167ft), is the highest village on the island. It also one of the oldest, pre-dating the Spanish conquest, and Artenara is its Guanche name. Many of the houses in the village are built into the solid rock, although some of them, with their painted facades, look like ordinary houses, and most have modern amenities. The cave church, **La Ermita de la Cuevita**, is only identified by a bell above the door. It houses the *Virgen de la Cuevita*, whose festival is celebrated at the end of August. The Iglesia de San Matías is a more conventional church.

Mirador La Cilla (see page 112) is on most visitors' itineraries, a cave restaurant entered via a long tunnel. It has a sunny terrace with magnificent views of Roque Bentaiga and Roque Nublo and the substantial island dishes – including *ropa vieja*, *papas arrugadas* and grilled meats – are good value.

Pinar de Tamadaba, high above the west coast

PINAR DE TAMADABA

From Artenara, a road leads around the **Pinar de Tamadaba 25**, 8 sq km (3 sq miles) of protected forest within a much larger nature park, where Canary pines (*Pinus canariensis*) grow to enormous heights, untroubled by pollution – some reach almost 60m (190ft). Forest fires occur periodically, but the pine is capable of rapid regeneration. There are footpaths through the forest but great care must be taken not to cause fires or in any way damage the environment. The road does not lead beyond the *pinar*, so you have to return the way you came.

BARRANCO DE FATAGA

If you are approaching the central peaks from the south, you should take the Fataga road from Playa del Inglés. This leads through the beautiful **Barranco de Fataga**, where burnished walls of rock are reminiscent of canyons in the American West. After an easy start, the bends in the road become tighter and the valley is greener. Palm trees line the road side and tropical fruits are cultivated on the valley floor.

Passing the popular Mundo Aborigen and the Camel Safari Park you soon arrive in the village of **Fataga**, perched precipitously on a rock jutting out into the gorge. There is a nice

Taking in Barranco de Fataga

church and several cheerful restaurants, some of them offering barbecues and live music, catering to visitors on jeep safaris from the coast.

The road winds towards **San Bartolomé de Tirajana** ㉖, an historic little town, the administrative centre of a region that includes Maspalomas and Playa del Inglés. The town's main source of income is the production of

> ### Mountain liqueurs
>
> The mountain regions specialise in liqueurs. *Guindilla* is a cherry liqueur made in San Bartolomé and takes its name from the Spanish word for morello cherries – *guindas*. *Mejunje* is a sweet concoction of rum, honey and lemon that was traditionally served to priests when they visited their parishioners.

fruit, especially cherries. The Ayuntamiento (Town Hall) has an attractive inner courtyard, and there are two churches – the neoclassical San Bartolomé, outside which a market is held on Sunday morning, and Santiago el Apóstol. The festival of Santiago (St James) is a major event on 25 July. You may want to stop at the petrol station here for fuel, as garages are few and far between in the mountains.

PICO DE LAS NIEVES AND ROQUE BENTAIGA

Following signs to Tejeda you will reach the little village of **Ayacata**, from where there is a popular and not too demanding walk to Roque Nublo, which takes about 40 minutes each way. It passes another, smaller, rock figure known as El Fraile (The Monk). If you look carefully you may (just) see a resemblance to a praying monk.

Off to the right a road wriggles round a reservoir, the Presa de los Hornos. Not far away is the **Centro de Interpretación Degollada de Bercerra** (daily 10am–5pm; free), an information centre with a *mirador* offering panoramic views. Looming above is the **Pico de las Nieves** ㉗, the highest peak on the

Santa Lucía's white facades

island, crowned by a radar station and tv transmitter. The summit is not accessible as it is used as a military base, but there is a lookout point not far below.

The road to the west from Ayacata, signposted to Bentaiga, is asphalted at first but soon becomes a gravel track. After Roque Nublo, **Roque Bentaiga** is the most spectacular monolith in the range. In 1483 it was the site of a fierce battle in which the Spaniards, led by Pedro de Vera, defeated the indigenous Guanches. A Guanche refuge, called the Cueva del Rey (King's Cave), lies at the foot of the outcrop. It is well worth stopping at the **Centro de Interpretación** (daily 10am–4pm, Sat–Sun until 6pm) to get some background information. From here, those with enough energy can scramble the last stretch to the peak.

FORTALEZA GRANDE AND SANTA LUCÍA

An alternative way to approach the central peaks is from the east, from Agüimes, via Santa Lucía on the GC-550 or from the Cruce de Sardina exit off the motorway (GC-65). It almost goes without saying that these are winding roads with sharp bends, but the scenery is spectacular, with prickly pears, euphorbia and olive trees gradually losing ground to bare, reddish rock.

Off to the left of the GC-65 you will see **Fortaleza Grande**, a rock uncannily shaped like a castle, which was one of the last refuges of the Guanches. Some of those who survived the defeat at Roque Bentaiga obeyed the command of their leader, Tenesor Semidan, to surrender; others, it is said, threw themselves from these cliffs.

Surrounded by pines, **Santa Lucía** ㉘ is a beautiful little village with blindingly white houses, bougainvillaea tumbling over walls, and an imposing domed church with a double bell-tower. There's a children's playground and a small museum, the **Museo Castillo de la Fortaleza** (daily 10.30am–5.30pm, Sat–Sun 11.30am–5.30pm) where Guanche artefacts, agricultural tools and a Roman amphora are displayed.

A final way to approach the peaks is via Moya or Arucas in the north. The road from Arucas is the better of the two, but the Moya route goes past the lovely Pinos de Gáldar pine forest. Both lead – circuitously, of course – to Cruz de Tejeda.

CAMINOS REALES

A series of ancient paths known as *caminos reales* – royal paths – have been restored and opened up to walkers as part of an attempt to promote conservation-conscious tourism and *senderismo* – hiking. These old tracks, once the only means of getting around the interior of Gran Canaria, centre on Cruz de Tejeda and radiate out to much of the island, from Maspalomas in the south to Agaete in the northwest. While some walks are demanding, others are relatively short and gentle. For more information, contact the Patronato de Turismo, Calle Triana 93, Las Palmas (tel: 928 219 600), or go to the helpful government bookshop, the Librería del Cabildo Insular, Calle Cano 24, Las Palmas (tel: 928 381 539) for maps and books in English.

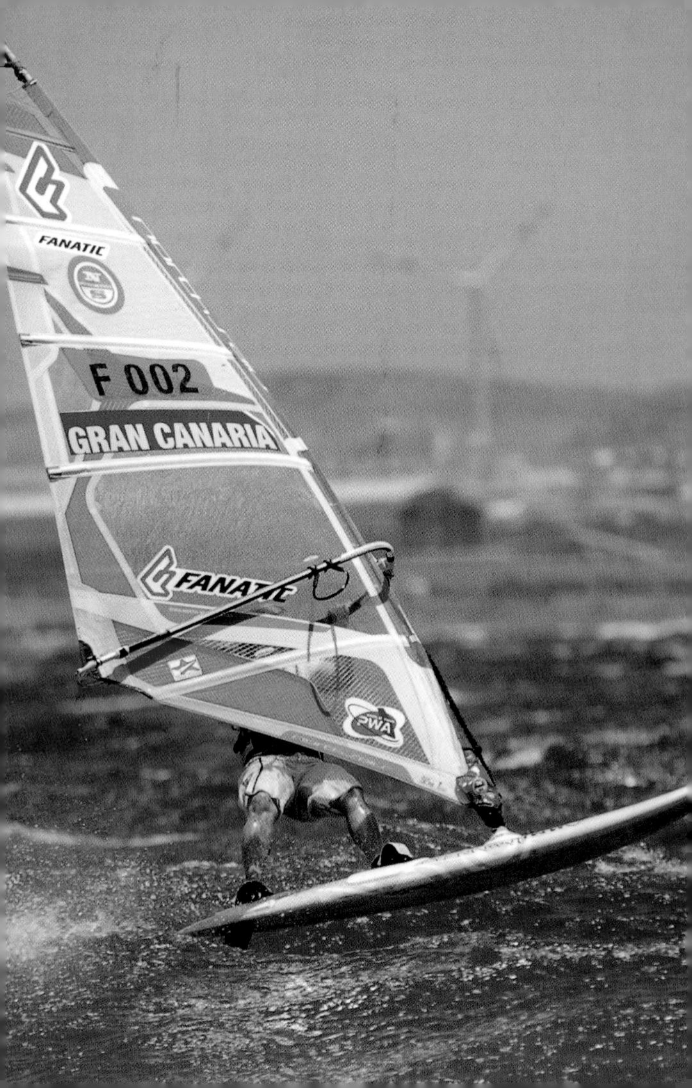
FANATIC
F 002
GRAN CANARIA
FANATIC
PWA

WHAT TO DO

SPORTS

The spectrum of sports and outdoor activities available on Gran Canaria runs from the mildly energetic to the extremely vigorous. While most of the activities take place on, in or under the water, there are many land-based pursuits, from hiking to horse riding and golf.

WINDSURFING

Gran Canaria is considered one of the best places in the world for windsurfing – some say only Hawaii beats it. It can be practised all along the coast running from Melenera in the east to Maspalomas in the south. At **Playa de Vargas** and **Pozo Izquierdo** near Arinaga, strong winds are constant all year round and waves always high. A little further south, near San Agustín, winds are good in Bahía Feliz and Playa del Águila.

The two best windsurf schools, which offer beginners' and advanced courses, are **Fanatic Boarders Center** (formerly Mistral Club), Playa de Trajalillo, Urbanización Bahía Feliz, tel: 928 157 158, http://fanaticboarderscenter.com, and **F2 Surfcenter Dunkerbeck**, Playa del Águila, San Agustín, tel: (45) 8686 1122, www.dunkerbeck-windsurfing.com (run by world champion Björn Dunkerbeck). Windsurfing conditions are also good on the Playa de las Canteras, Las Palmas and at Gáldar in the far northwest corner.

SURFING AND BODYBOARDING

The north of the island, between Las Palmas and Gáldar, is best for surfing and bodyboarding. Constant on-shore winds along this rocky coastline make ideal conditions for surfers and waves can be up to 5m (16ft) high. Conditions are also

Gran Canaria has excellent conditions for windsurfing

Exploring the reef

good around Arinaga, on the east coast, and between Playa del Inglés and Maspalomas in the south, where tuition and courses are offered by **PR Surfing**, Av. de Moya no. 6 Playa Del Ingles, C.C Eurocenter loc 80, tel: 628 104 025, www.prsurfing.com.

DIVING

There is a fascinating world beneath the waters off Gran Canaria and a number of excellent diving sites. In Las Palmas, where La Barra forms a giant aquarium, protected from the force of the waves, there is a wealth of underwater life to explore. On the east coast there is a diving centre at **Playa del Cabrón** where the diversity of fish and vegetation is so great that the area has been designated a marine reserve. **Pasito Blanco**, in the south near **Puerto Rico**, is another good spot, with ideal conditions for underwater photography, and there are two wrecks in the waters off this coast waiting to be explored (experienced divers only). In the northwest, **Sardina** is a popular spot for night dives into rocky depths of 17m (52ft).

Reputable diving schools with qualified instructors include: **Buceo Canarias Medusasub**, Calle Joaquin Blanco Torrent opposite dock H, Las Palmas, tel: 928 232 085, www.buceo canarias.com; **Centro Turístico de Submarinismo Sun Sub**, Plaza de Ansite s/n, Playa del Inglés, tel: 928 778 165, www.sunsub.com; **Davy Jones Diving**, Calle Luis Velasco 36-38, Playa de Arinaga, Aguimes, tel: 900 460 147, www.davyjones diving.com; and **Top Diving Puerto Escala**, Puerto Escala c. Doreste y Molina s/n, Puerto Rico, tel: 928 560 609, www.top diving.net. The latter has its own decompression chamber.

SAILING

Gran Canaria is a sailor's dream, especially from April to October. Winds are reliably good and the climate is excellent. The main centres are Las Palmas and the south coast, specifically Pasito Blanco, Arguineguín, Puerto Rico and Puerto de Mogán. The island attracts experienced sailors – members of Puerto Rico's sailing school have brought home five Olympic gold medals! – but it suits beginners too.

The annual Atlantic Rally for Cruisers (ARC; www.worldcruising.com) starts at the Muelle Deportivo in Las Palmas in Gran Canaria and makes the 2,700-nautical mile journey to St Lucia in the Caribbean.

Among many reliable sailing clubs and schools are: **Real Club Náutico**, Calle León

Boat trips

To experience the sea while someone else does the work, take a trip in a glass bottom boat run by Líneas Salmon (tel: 649 919 383, www.lineas salmon.es) or Líneas Bluebird (tel: 629 989 633/366; www.lineasbluebird.com) between the ports of Arguineguín, Puerto Rico and Puerto de Mogán. Or try the Super Cat from Puerto de Mogán (tel: 928 150 248; www.canary boattrips.com) for a lazy day on a sailing catamaran, with on-board barbecues.

y Castillo 308, Las Palmas, tel: 928 234 566, www.rcngc.com;
Real Club Victoria, Paseo de las Canteras 4, tel: 928 460 630,
www.realclubvictoria.com; Luis Molina **Escuela Deportiva
Náutica**, Playa de Anfi, Barranco de la Verga s/n, tel: 928 151
440; and the **Club Regatas Suroeste Mogán**, Pantalán 1 – Puerto
Escala, Puerto Rico, tel: 680 797 240; www.clubregatassuroeste.
com. For information on lateen sailing, contact the **Federación
de Vela Latina Canaria**, Muelle Deportivo, Las Palmas, tel: 928
230 616, www.federacionvelalatinadebotes.org.

DEEP-SEA FISHING

Gran Canaria is well-known for its game fishing and Pasito
Blanco, Puerto Rico and Puerto de Mogán are the major centres. Puerto Rico's fishermen are the proud holders of numerous world records in deep-sea fishing, but this is a sport in
which beginners can indulge, too. Several varieties of tuna
and marlin as well as swordfish and, sometimes, sharks can
be found in these well-stocked waters. The deep-sea fishing

LUCHA CANARIA AND JUEGO DEL PALO

Lucha canaria – Canary Islands wrestling – is the most popular traditional sport on the islands and can be seen at rural fiestas, in the
Estadio López Socas in Las Palmas, and in Gáldar. Two teams of 12
wrestlers take it in turns to face a member of the opposing team in
a sandy ring, with the aim of throwing the opponent to the ground.
After a maximum of three rounds (*bregas*) the winner is the team
that loses the fewest wrestlers. The game was practised in pre-
Hispanic times, when it may have had more serious overtones.

Juego del Palo (stick fighting) is another ancient rural sport, also
practised at fiestas. The object is to move the body as little as possible while attacking and fending off the blows of an opponent.

Sailing enthusiasts flock to the south coast

season is roughly from May to September, but there is bottom-fishing available all year round.

A number of organisations offer fishing trips that include lunch and equipment. Try **White Striker** (Puerto Rico, tel: 928 735 013; www.whitestriker.com), with a knowledgeable skipper and an arrangement with a café on the jetty to cook the smaller fish you bring back. Tuna is sold direct to restaurants; marlin is collected by staff from a children's home in Las Palmas. Also recommended in Puerto Rico is **Blue Marlin III** (tel: 607 626 237, www.bluemarlin3.com).

WALKING

There's lots to do on land, and the most popular activity is hiking – *senderismo*. This is being promoted by the Cabildo Insular as a way of diversifying the tourist industry and encouraging visitors to explore the interior of the island. More than 66,000 hectares (164,000 acres) of land in Gran Canaria is under some kind of protection order. There are rural parks,

The manicured greens at the Real Club de Golf de Las Palmas

nature reserves, fully protected reserves and natural monuments, and there is access to most of this land. A series of ancient paths, the *caminos reales*, or royal paths (see page 81), once the only means of traversing much of the island, have been opened up for walkers. There are some challenging walks and climbs in the mountainous centre of the island, but there are many other less strenuous routes as well.

A guidebook to these paths can be purchased in the bookshop of the **Cabildo Insular de Gran Canaria** (Calle Bravo Murillo 23, Las Palmas). Or contact the Patronato de Turismo (C/. Triana 93, Las Palmas, tel: 928 219 600, www.grancanaria.com), who publish a series of leaflets, including maps.

There are many great walks in the *barrancos*. For general information on organised hikes, contact **Grupo Montañero Gran Canaria** (Calle Guillermo Santana Rivero 1, Las Palmas, tel: 928 427 475, http://gmgrancanaria.es). For hikes with a knowledgeable guide in the Barranco de Guayadeque, contact **Caminos de Herradura** (Calle Méjico 11, Agüimes, tel: 928 789 099, email: caminoherradura@terra.es). **Free-Motion** (Sandy Beach Hotel, Avenida Alferéces Provisionales, Playa del Inglés, tel: 928 777 479, www.free-motion.com) also arrange hikes.

Whether you are in a group or not, remember the basics: strong, comfortable shoes, sunblock, sun hat, sweater or jacket for lower temperatures in the mountains, and something to cover exposed shoulders in the sun. Take plenty of drinking water with you – it's easy to get dehydrated.

GOLF

There are eight golf courses in Gran Canaria, three in the north and five in the south. They include the **Real Club de Golf de Las Palmas** (Santa Brígida, tel: 928 351 050, make online reservations at www.realclubdegolfdelaspalmas.com) with 18 holes, par 71. It sits on the rim of the Bandama volcanic crater and is the oldest club in Spain, founded by British expatriates in 1891. **Maspalomas Golf Club** (Avenida TTOO Neckermann s/n, tel: 928 762 581, www.maspalomasgolf.net) has 18 holes, par 73, and has also been operating for some years; **Salobre Golf Club** (Autopista gc-1, Km53 between Maspalomas and Puerto de Mogán, tel: 928 943 004; www.salobregolfresort.com) has two excellent 18-hole courses (north and south). For more information, visit the island's official website, www.grancanaria.com.

HORSE RIDING

The **Real Club de Golf** at Santa Brígida (tel: 928 351 050) has a riding school. Lessons and trekking are also available at the **Picadero Oasis de Maspalomas** (tel: 928 762 378) and **El Salobre Canyon Horse Farm** (Maspalomas, tel: 616 418 363; www.elsalobrehr.es), which arranges pick-ups from the southern resorts.

Jeep safaris are a good way to see the mountainous areas

FLYING, PARACHUTING AND SKY DIVING

To try flying or parachuting, contact the **Escuela Canaria de Parapente** (tel: 630 082 655), or the **Club de Parapente Sirocco** (tel: 606 424 685; www.parapentegran canariaclubsiroco.com) in Las Palmas. For sky diving – a flight over the Maspalomas dunes and a jump in tandem with an instructor from 3,000m (9,840ft) – contact **Paraclub Gran Canaria** (tel: 928 157 000, www.paraclub degrancanaria.com).

JEEP AND QUAD SAFARIS

Jeep safaris from Playa del Inglés to Fataga are popular. Most include a barbecue lunch in the price; some throw in a free video of your trip, others will sell you one. Try **Discovery Jeep Safari** (tel: 928 775 188, www.discoverysafari.es).

Quad safaris are only for the daring. They go off-road on the route to Fataga along river beds and rocky tracks. Contact **Free-Motion**, who also organise more easy-going bike tours and rent mountain bikes.

SHOPPING

Gran Canaria looks set to maintain its status as a Free Trade Zone for the foreseeable future, despite membership of the EU, and taxes (IGIC) are low, at 7 percent, so there are savings to be made on tobacco, spirits, perfume, cosmetics, watches, jewellery, and electronic and optical equipment in Las Palmas duty-free shops.

Handicraft items (*artesanía*), including textiles, baskets and ceramics, can be found in shops and markets all over the island, but the best quality goods are sold in the outlets of the **Fundación para la Etnografía y el Desarrollo de la Artesanía Canaria** (FEDAC; www.fedac.org). These are situated at Calle Domingo J. Navarro 7, Las Palmas, tel: 928 369 661, and in the tourist office in the Yumbo Centre, corner Avenida EEUU and Avenida de España, Playa del Inglés, tel: 928 772 445. The FEDAC shops also sell the small knives, once used by banana workers and shepherds, that have become collectors' items. Called *cuchillos canarios* or *naifes*, they have a wide blade and a goat horn handle decorated with inlaid patterns.

Calle Peregrina, just round the corner from FEDAC, has a few attractive little boutiques and galleries. The **Librería del Cabildo Insular** (the official government bookshop; Calle Cano 24, Las Palmas, tel: 928 381 539, http://libroscanarios.org) is the place for maps and books about all the Canary Islands.

In the big commercial zones of Las Palmas you will find all the major stores, Spanish and international. The biggest centres in and near Las Palmas are **Las Arenas** (near the Auditorio Kraus; a 15-minute drive), **La Ballena**, in the upper town, and the **Avenida Mesa y López**, which is known as a 'zona comercial', where there are two branches of

Unusual plants

The Gando airport shop has a wide selection of plants, from miniature dragon trees to *Strelitzia* (bird of paradise) flowers, as well as a variety of seeds. Whether or not they will grow in the English climate is a gamble, but they make unusual gifts – and there is no restriction on bringing them into the UK.

the biggest Spanish department store, El Corte Inglés. A newer centre, with a wide range of shops as well as cafés, restaurants, cinemas and discos, is **El Muelle**, on the Muelle Santa Catalina.

Among edible items, *queso de flor*, the famous cheese made in Guía, is a good choice. **La Quesera** (Calle Pérez Galdós 27, Santa María de Guía, tel: 928 553 326) is one of the best places to buy it. Jars of mojo sauce in many varieties and *bienmesabe* (the syrupy almond dessert) are widely available. **La Elvira** (Calle Juan Ramón Giménez 45, Mercado de Altavista puesto 15, Las Palmas, tel: 662 323 608) sells good-quality island wines as well as local and Latin American foods.

MARKETS

Most towns have a weekly market, selling food, flowers and household goods. There's a good one in **Puerto de Mogán**

A colourful stall at Vegueta food market

(Friday) and another in the San Fernando district of **Playa del Inglés** (Saturday). **San Mateo** has a huge farmers' market on Sunday morning. In Las Palmas, the slightly overpriced **Vegueta food market** is a riot of colours and smells every morning except Sunday, and surrounded by tiny, white-tiled bars; and on Sunday morning, a flower market is held in Plaza de Santa Ana. Head to Mercado Central (Calle Galicia 24, Mon–Sat, tel: 928 242 910) for a great variety of fresh vegetables, fruits, meats and fish at bargain prices.

NIGHTLIFE

Discos, clubs and bars rapidly fall in and out of favour. Very little happens before midnight, so a quiet place you pass at 10.30pm may be thumping two hours later. In Las Palmas, Plaza de España in the Mesa y López district is lively. **The Kitchen** at Calle Ruiz de Alda 17 is a perfect place to watch the sun go down sipping their legendary mojitos. The **Sotavento Club** at Muelle Deportivo (Calle Joaquín Blanco Torrent; http://sotaventoclub.com) is where the beautiful people go to dance the night away on the open-air terrace. Further south, the café tables in Plaza Hurtado de Mendoza are full till the early hours. **La Azotea de Benito** on Plaza de Hurtado Mendoza 1 boasts wonderful views from its roof terrace and excellent cocktails. Chester (Calle Simon Bolivar 3) also serves good cocktails.

There are hundreds of bars, clubs and discos in Playa del Inglés and Maspalomas. Flyers handed out in the street or listings in local papers will point the way. The commercial centres are the places to go. **Costa Chinawhite** in the **Kasbah Centre** is popular and has a good rota of international DJs, as does **Pachá Gran Canaria** on Calle Sargentos Provisionales (Playa del Inglés; http://pachagrancanaria.com). The **Yumbo Centre** is known for its gay bars and clubs (http://yumbocentrum.com).

Casinos: There are two: Casino Las Palmas in Las Palmas (Calle León y Castillo 324-326, tel: 928 234 882), the other one is in the Lopesan Costa Meloneras Resort (tel: 928 143 909). Dress smartly and don't forget your passport.

Classical music: The **Auditorio Alfredo Kraus** at the far end of Playa de las Canteras (www.auditorioteatrolaspalma sgc.es) presents excellent concerts by the resident Las Palmas Philharmonic and visiting orchestras, and recitals by top-class soloists. The **Teatro Cuyás** (Calle Viera y Clavijo s/n, Triana; www.teatrocuyas.com), stages world and classical music, dance and theatre, as does the **Teatro Pérez Galdós** (Plaza Stagno 1; www.auditorioteatrolaspalmasgc.es). **CICCA** (Alameda de Colón 1, tel: 928 368 687; www.lacajadecanarias. es) has a varied programme of films, music, modern dance and theatre.

CHILDREN'S GRAN CANARIA

Gran Canaria is a great place for children as there are numerous places to entertain them when they tire of the beach or the sun gets too much. Close to Playa del Inglés/Maspalomas, and with regular bus services, you will find:

Mundo Aborigen (daily 9am–6pm), Parque Rural de Ayagaures, Carretera de Fataga Km6, tel: 928 172 295, www.mundoaborigen.com. A great re-creation of a Guanche settlement, with life-size models. Adults usually enjoy it, too.

Camel Safari Park (daily 10am–6pm; www.camelsafarigran canaria.com), La Baranda, Carretera de Fataga, tel: 928 798 680. Camel treks, a shop and a restaurant are on offer here.

Palmitos Park (daily 10am–6pm), Barranco de los Palmitos, tel: 928 797 070, www.palmitospark.es. An ornithological park and botanical garden that also has dolphin shows.

Aqualand (daily 10am–5pm), Carretera Palmitos Park Km3, tel: 928 140 525, www.aqualand.es. The biggest water park in the Canaries, with slides and flumes of all descriptions.

Holiday World (daily 5.30–11pm, tel: 928 730 498), Maspalomas, www.holidayworld maspalomas.com) is another huge leisure park.

Sioux City (Tue–Sun 10am–5pm, plus Fri barbecue 8pm), Cañon del Águila, San Agustín, tel: 928 762 573, http://siouxcitypark.es. A Wild West theme park, complete with gunfights, bank hold-ups and saloon girls.

Submarine Adventure (daily 10am–5pm), Puerto de Mogán, tel: 928 565 108, http://atlantidasubmarine.

A slice of the Wild West at Sioux City

com, takes you on a 90-minute voyage to the bottom of the sea in a yellow submarine.

Cocodrilo Park (Sun–Fri 10am–5pm; www.cocodrilopark zoo.com), Los Corralillos, Agüimes, tel: 928 784 725. Parrots, monkeys and deer, as well as around 300 crocodiles.

In Las Palmas, children usually enjoy a trip around town on the open-topped **Guagua Turística** (tourist bus). You can hop on and off all day at places of interest.

Museo Elder (www.museoelder.org; Tue–Sun 10am–8pm), the big science and technology museum in Parque Santa Catalina, is a hit with children with its hands-on activities and a section especially designed for very young ones, as well as an IMAX cinema.

CALENDAR OF EVENTS

6 January: Epifanía del Señor (Epiphany). Children receive their Christmas presents. In Las Palmas the Three Kings (Los Reyes) ride into town, sometimes on camels, throwing sweets to the crowd.

February: Fiesta de Almendros (Almond Blossom Festival) in Tejeda and Valsequillo (date varies). Traditional handicrafts, dance and sports displays.

Late February/early March: Carnival. Celebrations are particularly outrageous in Las Palmas and Playa del Inglés. International Film Festival in Las Palmas, various locations

April: Semana Santa. The week preceding Easter is a time of solemn processions..

End April–early May: Cheese festival, Santa María de Guía. Traditional dancing and lots of local produce.

Mid-June: Corpus Christi. The streets of Vegueta and the Plaza de Santa Ana in Las Palmas, and main squares in Arucas and Gáldar, are carpeted with flowers, grasses and coloured sand.

24 June: San Juan (Feast of St John). Dancing, processions and sporting activities in Artenara, Telde, Las Palmas and Arucas.

16 July: Nuestra Señora del Carmen, the patron saint of fishermen, is honoured in all ports, but especially in Arguineguín and Puerto de Mogán. Statues of the Virgin are taken out to sea in processions of decorated boats.

4 August: Bajada de las Ramas (Bringing down the Branches) is held in Agaete and Puerto de las Nieves. The villagers carry branches from the mountains to the sea and whip the waves.

8 September: Virgen del Pino. Important festival in Teror, which is a mixture of religious rituals and secular fun.

11 September: Fiesta del Charco (Festival of the Lagoon) in Puerto de la Aldea, San Nicolás. Participants try to catch fish with their hands, and duck each other into the water.

Second Saturday in October: Fiestas de la Naval (Festival of the Sea). Maritime processions in Las Palmas and other ports celebrate the victory of the Armada over the English in 1595.

EATING OUT

Canary Islands' food has much in common with that of mainland Spain, but with interesting regional differences. There are also dishes similar to those found in parts of Latin America – although whether these recipes were introduced to the New World by Canarian emigrants, or American inventions brought back by returnees, is debatable.

You will also find many restaurants where the cooking is described as *cocina vasca* (Basque) or *cocina gallega* (Galician) because a number of cooks from these northern regions of Spain have opened restaurants on the island. Their familiarity with Atlantic fish and seafood may help them feel at home here. As these two regions have a reputation for some of the best cooking in Spain, they are a welcome addition.

Pork chops with mojo verde sauce

FISH

As you would expect on an Atlantic island, there is lots of fish and seafood of all kinds. Along with the ubiquitous *sardinas*, fresh from the ocean, the fish most commonly seen on menus are *cherne* (sea bass), *vieja* (parrot fish), *sama* (sea bream) and *bacalao* (salt cod). You will also find *merluza* (hake) *atún* (tuna) and *bonito* (a variety of tuna) and seafood such as *gambas* (prawns), *pulpo* (octopus), *calamares* (squid) and *almejas* (clams).

A selection of local tapas

Often, fish will be served simply grilled along with salad, *mojo* sauce and *papas arrugadas* – a perfectly balanced dish – but there are numerous other ways that it may appear on your table. *Sancocho canario* is a popular dish, a stew made with red grouper or sea bass, potatoes and yams, spiced up with a hot variety of *mojo* sauce. *Salpicón de pescado* is another dish you will see on many menus: this is sea bass or grouper cooked, chopped and served cold with a mixture of onions, garlic, tomatoes and peppers, topped with crumbled hard-boiled egg and olives. A delicacy introduced from the Basque country is *calamares rellenos de bacalao* – small squid with a tasty, cod-based stuffing, sometimes served in a creamy sauce.

MEAT

If you don't like fish, don't despair, there's plenty of meat to be found. *Cabrito* (kid) – sometimes called *baifo* – and *conejo* (rabbit) are most common, but pork (*cerdo*) and chicken (*pollo*) are popular and there are some good steaks to be had in restaurants catering to tourists. Both goat and rabbit are often served *al salmorejo* (with green peppers, in a herb and garlic marinade). *Chorizo*, the red spicy sausage found all over Spain, also crops up in a variety of guises.

SOUPS

Most of the world's traditional dishes originated as a way of filling stomachs with what was available and inexpensive. In the Canary Islands, this meant a whole range of substantial soups and stews. *Ropa vieja* (literally, old clothes) is a mixture of meat, tomatoes and chickpeas; *puchero* includes meat, pumpkin and any vegetables available; while *rancho canario* – mixing vermicelli with chickpeas, potatoes, bacon, chorizo and chicken – is the most elaborate and some say the best. Many of the soups contain chunks of corn on the cob. Vegetarians should note that even watercress soup (*potaje de berros*), a staple of many menus, has chunks of bacon in it. And celery soup (*potaje de apio*) may contain scraps of pork.

VEGETABLES

The vegetables you are offered will be those that are in season and because the island does not produce a great variety, and imports are expensive, choice may be limited. Pulses such as lentils (*lentejas*) and chickpeas (*garbanzos*) are used a lot; Canary tomatoes are delicious. If you like garlic, ask for *tomates aliñados*, tomato salad smothered with olive oil and garlic. *Pimientos de padrón* – small green peppers cooked whole and covered with salt – originated in Galicia and are now found everywhere. Avocados (strictly speaking a fruit not a vegetable) are served at a perfect stage of ripeness.

Most dishes contain or are accompanied by potatoes (*papas*), and sometimes by *ñame*, a kind of yam. You'll encounter *papas arrugadas* (wrinkled potatoes), which are

served with meat and fish or by themselves as tapas. They
are small potatoes – the yellow-fleshed Tenerife variety are
best – cooked in their skins in salted water then dried over a
low heat until their skins wrinkle and a salty crust forms. It is
said that this dish originated with fishermen who used to boil
the potatoes in seawater.

MOJO

Papas arrugadas, and many meat dishes, are usually accompanied by *mojo rojo*, a sauce whose basic ingredients are
tomatoes, peppers and paprika. A spicier version (*mojo picón*)
contains hot chili pepper as well. *Mojo verde* is a green sauce
made with oil, vinegar, garlic, coriander and parsley, usually served with fish. The sauces arrive at the table in small
bowls so you can use as much or as little as you like. Every
restaurant – and probably every home – seems to have their

The ubiquitous pimientos de padrón

own version and entire *mojo* recipe books are published.

GOFIO

Made of wheat, barley or a mixture of the two, *gofio* was the staple food of the Guanches and still forms

an essential part of the diet today – you even see sacks of *gofio para perros* (*gofio* for dogs). The cereal is toasted before being ground into flour and then has a multiplicity of uses. It is stirred into soups and into children's milk and used to thicken sauces. It is made into ice cream and mixed with oil, salt and sugar into a kind of bread, not unlike *polenta*. It is also blended with fish stock to make a thick soup called *gofio escaldado*.

CHEESE, FRUIT AND DESSERTS

There are only a few Canary Island cheeses, but they are delicious. The best known is a soft cheese, *queso de flor*, which is made in Guía, using a mixture of sheep and cows' milk curdled with the juice of flowers from the cardoon thistle, and has been awarded a Denomination of Origin. It has also won several World Cheese Awards, as has the *queso tierno de Valsequillo*, a mild, smooth cheese like mozzarella.

Home grown Canary Island fruit is delicious. As well as the small, local bananas there are papayas, guavas, mangoes and oranges, delicious by themselves, made into juice or used to flavour ice cream. On many menus desserts are limited to ice cream (*helado*), *flan* (the ubiquitous caramel custard), fresh fruit, and the one you see everywhere, *bienmesabe*, which translates as 'tastes good to me' – and so it does. There are numerous recipes, but basically it is a mixture of crushed almonds, lemon, sugar (lots), cinnamon and egg yolks.

WHAT TO DRINK

The breakfast drink is coffee. *Café solo* is a small, strong black, like an *espresso*; a *cortado*, served in a glass, is a shot of coffee with a small amount of hot milk; *café con leche* is a large milky coffee. An *Americano* is a shot of coffee with added hot water. Hot chocolate is sometimes available for breakfast, but if you ask for tea you will just get a teabag in a little pot.

The local cheeses are delicious

You are advised not to drink tap water, but *agua mineral* is available everywhere – *con gas* is sparkling, *sin gas* is still. *Zumo de naranja*, freshly-squeezed orange juice, is widely available and in some bars and cafés you can get more exotic juices.

Wine is usually drunk with meals, most of it imported from the mainland; Rioja is one of the favourites. There are 32 wineries on Gran Canaria, which has a recently introduced Denomination of Origin (DOC), but they come nowhere near to supplying demand. Monte Lentiscal, which has its own DOC, is the most widely available local wine. Tenerife is a bigger producer, but its wines are not regularly found in restaurants.

When Arucas had a thriving sugar industry it also used to be a centre of rum production. There is still a distillery there, the Destileria Arehucas (www.arehucas.es), producing excellent rum, but sugar has to be imported now so the output is much reduced. Rum forms the basis of *Mejunje*, a local drink in which the spirit is blended with honey and lemon. Another speciality is *Guindilla*, the cherry liqueur made in San Bartolomé.

Beer is extremely popular on the island. You will see familiar Spanish brands such as San Miguel, and other imported beers are available, but the most popular is the locally produced Tropical.

WHERE TO EAT

When it comes to places to eat, the choice is wide. There are some up-market restaurants in Las Palmas and Maspalomas that can compete with those in any capital city, and are not expensive by northern European standards. There are fishermen's *tavernas* where the fish is likely to be fresh and wholesome, with few trimmings; and rural *parrillas* – grills – where all kinds of meat and sausage are barbecued over an open fire and served with generous helpings of *papas arrugadas* and *mojo rojo*.

A *piscolabis* is a snack bar serving a variety of little sandwiches and snacks. When you see restaurants advertising *cocina casalinga* – home-cooking – you'll get inexpensive, typically Canarian food, although the quality, of course, can vary. There are not many places that style themselves tapas bars, but in many middle-of-the-range and inexpensive restaurants there will be a variety of tapas on offer, and some of the portions are quite large – two or three would make a meal for most people.

Bars, generally, are places in which to drink, not eat, although most will have croissants or pastries to accompany the morning coffee, some may serve sandwiches (*bocadillos*) or a limited range of tapas. A *kiosco* has the same role and

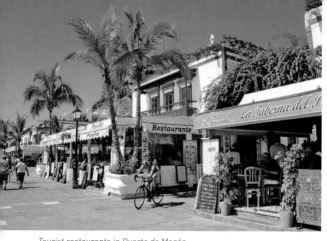
Tourist restaurants in Puerto de Mogán

these little kiosks can be found in the main squares of most towns and villages.

WHEN TO EAT

The islanders, like the people of mainland Spain, eat late. Three o'clock is not an unusual time to sit down to lunch, and ten o'clock is a relatively early hour to start dinner. Some restaurants may close for a few hours between lunch and dinner, but many serve food all day. Those who cater mostly to foreign visitors, aware that habits are different, will have their lunch menus out by midday and serve dinner as early as you like.

Sunday lunch is a major event in Gran Canaria and as this continues throughout the afternoon many restaurants are closed on Sunday evening. Some also close one evening during the week. Because the high season runs between November and April, and restaurateurs need to take a holiday, some close completely for three or four weeks in mid-summer.

TO HELP YOU ORDER

Could we have a table, please? **¿Nos puede dar una mesa, por favor?**

Do you have a set menu? **¿Tiene un menú del día?**

I would like... **Quisiera...**

The bill, please **La cuenta, por favor**

MENU READER

à la plancha grilled
agua mineral mineral water
al ajillo in garlic
arroz rice
asado roast
atún tuna
azúcar sugar
bacalao cod
bocadillo sandwich
boquerones anchovies
buey/res beef
calamares squid
callos tripe
cangrejo crab
cerdo pork
cerveza beer
champiñones mushrooms
cocido stew
cordero lamb
ensalada salad
entremeses hors d'oeuvre
flan caramel custard

helado ice cream
jamón serrano cured ham
judías beans
langosta lobster
leche milk
mariscos shellfish
mejillones mussels
morcilla black pudding
pan bread
pescado fish
picante spicy
poco hecho rare
pollo chicken
postre dessert
pulpitos baby octopus
queso cheese
sal salt
salsa sauce
ternera veal
tortilla omelette
trucha trout
verduras vegetables
vino wine

PLACES TO EAT

We have used the following symbols to give an idea of the price for a three-course meal for one, including wine, cover and service:

€€€€ over 60 euros   €€ 25–40 euros
€€€ 40–60 euros   € below 25 euros

LAS PALMAS

Deliciosa Marta €€ *Perez Galdos, 23, Las Palmas, tel: 928 370 882.* Arguably the best restaurant in Las Palmas: great food, friendly staff and a lovely romantic ambience. Lamb shoulder and steak tartare are both highly recommended. Advance booking essential.

El Apartamento €€ *Avenida Mesa y López, 1, tel: 828 014 33*, http://elapartamento.net. A trendy place with an eclectic menú of pastas, tagines, various *bocadillos* and excellent fish & chips. The modern interior is cosy, with comfy sofas near the windows. Closed Sunday in summer.

El Cerdo Que Ríe €€ *Paseo de las Canteras 31, tel: 928 271 731.* Established in the 1960s when northern European tourists first came to Las Palmas, the Danish-owned 'Laughing Pig' is still extremely popular. Its large menu, written up outside the restaurant, has strong, but not exclusive, Scandinavian leanings.

El Herreño €€ *Calle Medizábal 5, tel: 928 310 513.* Close to the Vegueta market, this busy restaurant is a Las Palmas institution. It serves hearty, simple food from the island of El Hierro, in a relaxed and friendly atmosphere. Large families sit at long tables to enjoy thick seafood stews followed by *gofio* mousse and *bienmesabe*.

El Padrino €€€ *Calle Jesús Nazareno 1, tel: 928 462 094*, www.restaurantelpadrino.es. This fish restaurant on La Isleta is famous not only for its seafood specialities, but also for marvellous views. Eat indoors or outside in a kind of marquee. Recommended for Sunday lunch, when it is wise to book.

El Patio del Cuyás €–€€ *Teatro Cuyás, Calle Viero y Clavijo s/n, Triana, tel: 928 384 800,* www.teatrocuyas.com. Part of a theatre in Triana, El Patio has recently reopened after renovation. The food is prepared by a well-regarded young chef and shows influences from the many parts of northern Spain in which he has worked. Book for lunch. Closed Monday, Tuesday and Wednesday evenings and Sunday.

Embarcadero €€€ *Club Marítimo Varadero, Muelle Deportivo, tel: 928 233 067,* http://restauranteembarcadero.com. In this smart waterfront restaurant the scallops with asparagus and smoked Hierro cheese are one of the star turns. Great location and good choice of wines.

Kitchen Lovers €€€ *Paseo de las Canteras 16, tel: 928 987 610.* A cosy, romantic waterfront restaurant with splendid seaviews and fine international cuisine – fresh seafood, Italian pasta and ingenious salads all feature on the menu.

La Marinera €€ *Alonso Ojeda, Paseo de las Canteras La Puntilla, tel: 928 461 555/928 468 802,* www.restaurantelamarineralaspalmas.com. At the end of Playa de las Canteras, this restaurant has a dining room so close to the sea that you could almost catch the fish yourself. Fortunately, they do it for you, and cook it extremely well. Barbecued meats are also on offer, as are a number of Canary Island wines.

Racimo 16 € *Lucas Fernández Navarro, 55, Las Palmas, tel: 673 242 002.* This cafeteria may be simple but it uses the freshest organic produce. The menu changes daily but there is always a fish, meat and vegetarian dish to choose from. Ideal for lunch as a set menu will only set you back €10.

Ribera del Río Miño €€€ *Calle Olof Palme, 21, Las Palmas, tel: 928 264 431,* www.riberadelriomino.com. Despite being expensive, this smart restaurant close to Playa de las Canteras and Plaza España has quickly become very popular. Recommended for its Galician cuisine and good wines.

THE EAST

AGÜIMES

Moorea Cocina Taller y Gastrobar €€€ *Avenida de Los Pescadores 63, tel: 928 188 851.* Be tempted by the innovative dishes from one of the most remarkable young Canarian chefs, Joaquin Espejo. The soft shell lobster is amazing. The interior is modern minimalist and there's a beautiful seaview to boot.

SANTA BRÍGIDA

Bodegón Vandama €€€ *Carretera Bandama, 116, tel: 928 352 754,* www.bodegonvandama.com. This charming tavern is off the beaten track and the better for it. Surrounded by vineyards and gardens, its speciality is the *parrilla* (grilled meats) served with tasty salsas, pimienta or Roquefort, and a glass of house wine. Closed Monday and Tuesday, Sunday lunch only .

TELDE

La Marisqueria La Rubia €€ *Calle Luis Morote, 47, tel: 928 132 223.* Arguably the best seafood restaurant in Telde, and therefore often gets very busy. Do not be deterred by the décor, as the food is excellent and the choice of *mariscos* amazing. It's good value too. No bookings. Closed in November.

THE SOUTH

MASPALOMAS

La Casa Vieja €–€€ *Calle el Lomo 139, Carretera de Fataga, tel: 928 769 010.* Traditional food served in an old country house with rustic decor and cane-lined walls, just a short taxi ride from the tourist centres. Barbecued meat and goat stews are among their specialities.

La Palmera del Sur €€€ *Calle Placido Domingo 12, Bellavista, San Fernando, tel: 659 598 003.* This small restaurant is not easy to find, but your efforts will be rewarded as the food is fantastic. The ever-changing menu features local and international dishes all using the best of ingredients. Great choice of wine. Closed Monday and Sunday.

La Proa Casa Reyes Meloneras €€ *Centro Comercial Meloneras Playa, Local 103, tel: 928 142 403*. This smart restaurant, with its excellent location and fantastic sea views, is also great value. The fresh fish and seafood are the highlight here.

Samsara €€ *Avenida del Oasis 30, Maspalomas, tel: 928 142 736*, www. samsara-gc.com. This Asian restaurant is an ideal location for a romantic evening. The menu is mostly Asian fusion and the tuna and duck carpaccios are delicious. Advance booking recommended.

MOGÁN

Acaymo €€ *Calle El Tostador 14, tel: 928 569 263*. In an attractive rustic building that was once a village school, Acaymo serves traditional island dishes, fish stews and good roast meats with *mojo* sauce.

Casa Enrique €–€€ *Calle San José 3, tel: 928 569 542*. Big, rather old-fashioned looking place in the main street where the proprietor serves local food such as *puchero* and *rancho canario* as well as plain grilled fish and steaks.

PLAYA DEL INGLÉS

La Compostela €€ *Avenida Tenerife 6, tel: 928 762 092/928 763 344*, www.compostelaplayadelingles.com. The emphasis at the Hotel Green Field restaurant is on food from Galicia. Specialities include *merluza a la Bilbaina* (hake, Bilbao style). Closed Monday.

Las Cumbres €€ *Avenida de Tirajana 11, tel: 928 760 941*. This long-standing favourite is decorated with old agricultural and domestic utensils. It specialises in dishes from various regions of Spain, particularly slow-roasted lamb, splendid Iberian hams and prawns from Huelva. Closed Tuesday and all of May.

Taberna La Caña €€ *Avenida Tenerife 4, tel: 928 761 553*, http:// tabernalacana.es. A family-friendly restaurant, with a children's menu, a few streets back from the beach, serving reliably good Mediterranean food. Full meals and tapas available. Makes a good paella.

Tenderete II €€ *Edificio Aloe, Avenida de Tirajana 15, tel: 928 767 180*, www.restaurantetenderete.com. On the ground floor of an apartment block, this does not look much from outside, but has been consistently good and popular for many years. Specialises in island dishes such as *puchero* and *rancho canario*. Reservations recommended. Closed Sunday.

PUERTO DE MOGÁN

La Cofradía €€ *Dársena Exterior s/n, tel: 928 565 321*, http://cofradiadepescadores.com. A local favourite on the fishermen's quay, where the fish comes straight off the boats. Busy and fun at Sunday lunchtime. If you're splashing out, go for the *cazuela de langosta* (lobster casserole).

Patio Canario €, *Urbanización Puerto de Mogán, tel. 928 565 456*. Overlooking the harbour, this friendly, faintly rustic restaurant serves fresh fish and local specialities, and is a lovely place to sit and watch the boats. Best value is the catch of the day, served grilled and with vegetables.

Qué tal by Stena €€ *Puerto de Mogán, tel: 928 56 55 34*, http://quetalbystena.com. Open for dinner only. This charming establishment prizes itself for its simple, beautifully presented dishes, some are even prepared in front of the customers.

PUERTO RICO

Picasso €€ *Calle Timanfaya 15, tel: 928 560 041*, www.restaurantepicasso.com. You will need to get a taxi as it's right at the top of the hill, near Apartamentos Lara. The menu features mainly seafood, fish and steaks, all well prepared and good value. Evenings only.

Red Rose €€ *Puerto Nuevo, tel: 928 562 185*. No view of the port although it's only a stone's throw away. Specials such as duck with orange sauce and lobster and seafood platter must be ordered 24 hours in advance. Open for breakfast, lunch and dinner and anything in between. It's popular with the English ex-pat community.

THE WEST AND NORTH

AGAETE

Huerto de Las Flores €–€€ *Huertas 1, tel: 608 149 011*. This cafeteria-style eatery may not look very sophisticated and it's true the big draw here are the botanic gardens themselves. The specialty of the house is the Agaete coffee, accompanied by a selection of cupcakes and other tempting sweets.

ARUCAS

El Chimenea €€€ *Carretera Arucas–Teror, Km12, tel: 651 643 944*. http://restaurantelachimenea.blogspot.com. On the main road outside town, El Chimenea has an interesting menu with mixed Canarian and Basque influences, and offers a range of local cheeses and wines. Closed Mon–Wed.

PUERTO DE LAS NIEVES

Las Nasas €€ *Calle Nuestra Señora de las Nieves 6, tel: 928 898 650*. One of many fish restaurants overlooking the port, Las Nasas has a cavernous dining room and terrace. They make a version of *ropa vieja* with octopus (*pulpo*). Popular with Las Palmas weekend visitors.

Ragú €€ *Paseo de los Poetas 10, Puerto de las Nieves, tel: 605 453 965*. One of the best seafood restaurants in this little port. On the menu you'll find octopus salad, fresh fish and shrimps. Note that it sometimes closes for private events.

TEROR

El Secuestro €–€€ *Avenida Cabildo Insular 26, tel: 928 630 231*. A reliable *parrilla* where they barbecue every kind of meat or sausage imaginable amid a rustic decor in a cheerful atmosphere. Fun at Sunday lunch time. Closed Sunday evening and Monday.

THE CENTRE

ARTENARA

Mirador La Cilla €, *Camino la Cilla 9, tel: 928 666 108.* This is the famous cave restaurant, with spectacular views from its sunny terrace, and kitchens cut into the rock. It serves typical, robust meat dishes, many with *mojo* sauce. Closes at sunset.

SAN MATEO

Restaurant 1801 €€€ *Avenida de Tinamar 8, tel: 928 661 126.* Named after the date the town was founded, this is a smart but welcoming restaurant, with an adventurous menu that includes duck in dry sherry sauce, and has an excellent wine list. Closed Monday, Tuesday and Sunday evening.

SANTA LUCÍA

El Mirador de Santa Lucia €€€ *Calle Maestro Enrique Hernández, n 5, tel: 928 798 005,* www.elmiradorsantalucia.com. This spacious, recently renovated restaurant serves up hearty, local dishes such as *salpicón de marisco* o *garbanzada* but the biggest draw here is without a doubt the view of the *barranco* below.

TEJEDA

Asador Grill Yolanda €–€€ *Cruz de Tejeda, tel: 928 666 276,* www. asadoryolanda.com. Next door to El Refugio, this is a smaller place that also serves good-value *asados* (roast meats) as well as salads, soups, sandwiches and good Canarian wines. A small covered terrace gives views of Tenerife's El Teide on a clear day. Closes around 8pm, when most visitors have left the area.

El Refugio € *Cruz de Tejeda, tel: 928 666 513/515,* www.hotelruralel refugio.com. In the hotel of the same name. You can eat indoors or on the roof terrace. Roast meats, such as goat and rabbit, are specialities but there are also good salads if you want a lighter meal. Excellent value and superb views across the mountains.

A–Z TRAVEL TIPS

A Summary of Practical Information

ACCOMMODATION

Accommodation on Gran Canaria is concentrated mainly in Las Palmas and in large, modern hotels in the southern resorts. Elsewhere, there is not a great deal of choice. You will not find budget accommodation in the resorts. In Puerto Rico, there are at present no hotels, only apartments and 'aparthotels'.

Hotels are rated from one-star to five-star Gran Lujo (GL). Ratings depend largely on facilities; prices within the categories may vary considerably. Breakfast is usually included in the basic rate in resort hotels and larger establishments. Package holidays are most economical, offering accommodation in large, comfortable hotels, usually with pools, and in self-catering apartments. Even if you don't want to spend your holiday in the resorts, they can provide a convenient base. Many hotels have adults-only and/or minimum-stay policies.

There are also apartments and 'aparthotels', where each room has kitchen facilities yet retains all the trappings of a hotel. Apartments are graded with one to four 'keys' depending on amenities. It is wise to book accommodation in advance, especially during the two high seasons – November to April and July to August.

In the interior there is a growing number of *casas rurales* – rural properties or old town houses that have been converted into small, medium-priced hotels or renovated and rented as self-catering accommodation. Contact Gran Canaria Rural (Calle Tenerife 24, Las Palmas, tel: 928 462 547/928 464 464, www.grancanariarural.com).

I would like a single/ double room **Quisiera una habitación sencilla/doble**
With/without bathroom and toilet/shower **con/sin baño/ducha**
What's the rate per night? **¿Cuál es el precio por noche?**
Is breakfast included? **¿Está incluído el desayuno?**

AIRPORT

Gando airport is on the east coast, about 20km (12 miles) south of Las Palmas. Bus No. 60 goes to Las Palmas (Parque San Telmo and Parque Santa Catalina terminals) at 15 and 50 minutes past the hour (6.15am to 11.15pm). The journey takes about 30 minutes and currently costs €2.95. There is also an hourly bus (No. 66) to Maspalomas between 7.20am and 8.20pm (journey time 30–40 minutes, cost €4.05), although most visitors going to the resorts will be on package holidays and will be collected at the airport by their tour operator. A taxi from the airport to Las Palmas (San Telmo) costs about €29, to Parque Santa Catalina about €33.

Gando airport: tel: 902 404 704 (24 hours), www.aena.es.

B

BICYCLE HIRE

Bikes can be hired in the resorts. Try Happy Biking, Centro Comercial Gran Chaparral, Playa del Inglés; www.happy-biking.com. For top-notch mountain and road bikes, go to Free Motion, Sandy Beach Hotel, Avenida Aleféreces Provisionales 6-8, Playa del Inglés, tel: 928 777 479, www.free-motion.com.

BUDGETING FOR YOUR TRIP

Gran Canaria is relatively inexpensive compared with many European destinations. To give you an idea of what to expect, here's a list of some average prices in euros.

Accommodation. Rates for two sharing a double room can range from as low as €40 at a *pensión* or *hostal* to as much as €400 at a top-of-the-range 5-star hotel. A pleasant 3-star hotel will cost in the range of €80–100. Rates drop considerably out of season – May to June and September to October are the least expensive, and are very pleasant months to be there.

Attractions. Most museums charge a small entry fee of around

€4–5. More expensive are the larger attractions such as Palmitos Park (€30 adults, €22 children); Aqualand (€28 adults, €19 children; both venues cheaper if you buy online); Cocodrilo Park (€9.90 adults, €6.90 children).

Buses. Single trips in Las Palmas, €1.40. Buying a rechargeable *BonoGuagua* Sin Contacto cuts the price by about a third. Bus from Playa del Inglés to Las Palmas, about €8 return.

Car hire. Including comprehensive insurance and tax, rates are around €40 a day from the big international companies; you get a better deal if you book for a week. Cars booked in advance online may be considerably cheaper (see Car Hire).

Getting there. Air fares vary enormously; those from the UK range between £160 and £600 (€210–€790). You get the best deals May–June and Sept–Oct. From the US, flights cost around $1,000 (€1000). Cheapest flights are usually available online.

Meals and drinks. In a bar a continental breakfast (fresh orange juice, coffee and toast or croissant), will cost around €5. The cheapest three-course set meal – the *menú del día* – including one drink, will be around €8–10. The average price of a three-course à la carte meal, including house wine, will be about €25 per person. At the top restaurants you may pay nearly twice that.

Petrol. Prices fluctuate, but are around €1 a litre.

Taxis. Prices are controlled, and reasonable. From the airport to Las Palmas the fare is around €30. Most trips within the city, and around Playa del Inglés, don't cost more than €5.

C

CAMPING

There are a number of free government-run campsites, called *zonas de acampada*, on the island, usually in attractive and sometimes remote places. You must get a permit from OIAC, Calle Agustín Millares Carló, Las Palmas, tel: 928 219 229; www.grancanaria.com.

CAR HIRE (see also Driving)

You must be over 21, sometimes 24, to hire a car, and to have held a licence for at least 24 months. You need your passport and a credit card. There are dozens of local companies, especially in Playa del Inglés, and these tend to be cheaper. It is also cheaper to hire a car online; **CICAR (Canary Islands Car)**, tel: 928 822 900, www.cicar. com, has been operating for over 30 years. Autos Moreno is a tried and tested local company (tel: 928 268 480, www.autosmoreno.es). All the big international companies have offices at the airport, in Las Palmas and in the resorts.

Airport offices: Avis tel 928 092 313, www.avis.es; Europcar tel: 928 574 292, www.europcar.es; Hertz tel: 928 579 577, www.hertz.es.

I'd like to rent a car for one day/week. **Quisiera alquilar un coche por un día/una semana.**
Please include full insurance. **Haga el favor de incluir el seguro a todo riesgo.**

CLIMATE

In the south sunshine is practically guaranteed all year round. Winter temperatures average 22–24ºC (72–75˚F), summer averages are 26–28ºC (79–82˚F), although they often exceed 30ºC (86˚F). It can be very windy, even in the hottest months. In the north of the island, temperatures are a few degrees lower and there is more cloud. Higher regions of the mountainous interior, of course, are much cooler. Some rain falls from Nov–Jan and in April, but showers are usually short.

CLOTHING

Light summer clothes, sandals and a swimsuit are all you need for much of the time, but bring a sweater or jacket for cooler evenings and for trips to the mountains, and strong shoes if you want to do any walking. A jacket and tie for men and a smart dress for women is appreciated, but not obligatory, in more expensive restaurants. Don't offend local sensibilities by wearing swimwear or skimpy clothing in city streets, museums or churches.

CRIME AND SAFETY

Crime rates are not high, but there is quite a lot of opportunistic bag-snatching and pick-pocketing in tourist areas, especially at markets or fiestas. Robberies from cars are most prevalent, so never leave anything of value in a car. If you have one, use the safe deposit box in your room for valuables, including your passport (carrying a photocopy of your passport is a good idea). Burglaries of holiday apartments occur, too, so keep doors and windows locked when you are out. Report all thefts to the police within 24 hours for your own insurance purposes.

I want to report a theft. **Quiero denunciar un robo.**

D

DISABLED TRAVELLERS

Gando airport and most modern hotels have wheelchair access and facilities for travellers with disabilities, as do the newer museums. For general information, consult the *Able Magazine* (Pentagon Centre, 36-38 Washington Street, Glasgow G3 8AZ, tel: 0141 285 4000, www.ablemagazine.co.uk). Tourism for All (tel: 0845 124 9971, www.tourismforall.org.uk) also provides information for travellers with disabilities. Also check the Canary government site http://gran canariaaccesible.info for the most up-to-date information.

DRIVING

Driving conditions. The rules are the same as in continental Europe: drive on the right, pass on the left, yield right of way to vehicles coming from your right. Coastal and mountain roads can be extremely sinuous and full of hairpin bends. In rural areas you may meet a herd of goats, a donkey cart, a large pothole or falling rocks.

Speed limits. 120 km/h (74 mph) on motorways, 100 km/h (62 mph) on dual carriageways, 90 km/h (52mph) on country roads, 50 km/h (31 mph) in built-up areas and 20 km/h (13mph) in residential areas.

Motorways. Toll-free.

Traffic and parking. In most towns traffic can be heavy, one-way systems confusing, and road signs inadequate. Early afternoon is a good time to get in and out of towns, and to find a parking space. It is an offence to park facing the traffic. Don't park on white or yellow lines. Blue lines indicate pay-and-display parking areas.

Petrol. Petrol is much cheaper than in the UK and the rest of Europe but prices have risen. Unleaded petrol is sin plomo. Some larger petrol stations are open 24 hours and most accept credit cards. In the mountainous centre there are very few petrol stations.

Rules and regulations. Always carry your driving licence with you. It is a good idea to have a photocopy of your passport. Seat belts are compulsory. Children under 10 must travel in the rear. Using mobile phones or GPS devices while driving is illegal.

Aparcamiento Parking
Desviación Detour
Obras Road works
Peatones Pedestrians
Peligro Danger
Salida de camiones Truck exit
Senso único One way
Useful expressions:
¿Se puede aparcar aquí? Can I park here?
Llénelo, por favor. Fill the tank please.
Ha habido un accidente. There has been an accident.

Traffic police. Armed civil guards (Guardia Civil) patrol the roads on motorcycles. In towns municipal police handle traffic control. If you are fined for a traffic offence, you may have to pay on the spot.

E

ELECTRICITY
220 volts is standard, with two-pin sockets. Adapters are available in UK shops and at airports. 110V appliances need a transformer.

EMBASSIES AND CONSULATES
UK: Calle Luís Morote 6, Las Palmas, tel: 928 262 508.
US: Calle Martínez Escobar 3, Oficina 7, Las Palmas, tel: 928 222 552.
Ireland: Calle León y Castillo 195, Las Palmas, tel: 928 297 728.
South Africa: Calle Albareda 54, Las Palmas, tel: 928 265 452.

If you lose your passport or run into trouble with the authorities or the police, contact your consulate for advice.

Where is the American/British consulate? **¿Dónde está el consulado americano/británico?**

EMERGENCIES (see also Embassies, Health and Police)
General emergencies: 112
National Police: 091
Local Police: 092
Guardia Civil: 062
Ambulance: 061
Fire Brigade: 080

Police! **Policía!**   Fire! **Fuego!**
Help! **Socorro!**   Stop! **Deténgase!**

G

GAY AND LESBIAN TRAVELLERS

Playa del Inglés is very gay-friendly. The Yumbo Centre is the main spot for bars and clubs, with about 40 aimed at the gay scene. There's a Gay Pride Festival in mid-May. Visit http://gaymaspalomas.com for more information.

GETTING THERE

By air. There are numerous direct budget airline flights from all UK airports to Gran Canaria. The flight time is 4–4.5 hours. Iberia, the Spanish national carrier (tel: 902 400 500, www.iberia.com) and British Airways (tel: 0870 850 9850, www.britishairways.com), fly via Madrid, which obviously takes longer. Check the web and advertisements in Sunday papers for good flight-only deals, but all-in package holidays can be the cheapest way to go.

At present there are several direct flights from the US (New York, Los Angeles, Chicago) operated by British Airways, Iberia, Norwegian (www.norwegian.com), Condor (www.condor.com) and Lufthansa (www.lufthansa.com). Other flights go via Madrid or Barcelona, or via London airports; check with a travel agency, or visit www.opodo.com. Both Ryanair (www.ryanair.com) and easyJet (www.easyjet.com) operate regular flights from London and other British airports.

Inter-island flights are operated by Binter Airlines (tel: 902 391 392, www.bintercanarias.com).

By ship. Trasmediterránea runs a weekly service from Cádiz to Las Palmas, which takes at least two days, and also operates services from Tenerife, Fuerteventura and Lanzarote to Las Palmas. For details, tel: 902 454 645; or www.trasmediterranea.es.

The Fred Olsen Shipping Line (tel: 902 100 107, www.fredolsen.es) runs ferries from Gran Canaria to Tenerife six times a day from Puerto de las Nieves (near Agaete) (journey time about 70 minutes; free bus from Parque Santa Catalina in Las Palmas). Naviera

Armas (tel: 902 456 500 or 928 227 311, www.naviera-armas.com) also has regular services to Tenerife, Fuerteventura and Lanzarote. The crossing to Tenerife takes about 2.5 hours.

HEALTH AND MEDICAL CARE

Non-EU visitors should always have private medical insurance, and although there are reciprocal arrangements between EU countries, it is advisable for people from the UK and other member nations to do the same, because not all eventualities are covered. The ehic card, which entitles EU citizens to free health care, is available in the UK from post offices or online at www.ehic.org.uk. Before being treated it is essential to establish that the doctor or service is working within the Spanish Health Service, otherwise you will be sent elsewhere.

Dental treatment is not available under this reciprocal system. Hotel receptionists or private clinics will recommend dentists.

There are two main hospitals in Las Palmas: the **Hospital Insular** (Plaza Dr Pasteur, Avenida Marítima del Sur, tel: 928 444 000) and the new **Hospital Dr Negrin** (Barranco de la Ballena, just off the GC-23 to the south of the city, tel: 928 450 000). The **Red Cross** (Cruz Roja) is based at Calle León y Castillo 231, Las Palmas, tel: 928 290 000.

In the resorts there are numerous private clinics where you will have to pay for treatment on the spot and reclaim it on your medical insurance. The Las Palmeras chain has clinics in Maspalomas, Playa del Inglés and San Agustín, tel: 928 762 993. In Puerto Rico, the British Medical Clinic (Avenida Tomás Roca Bosch 4, tel: 928 560 016) is reliable. In an emergency call 112, or 061 for an ambulance.

Most problems visitors experience are due to too much sun, too much alcohol or food that they are unused to – problems that can often be dealt with by **farmácias** (chemists/drugstores). Spanish pharmacists are highly trained and can often dispense medicines over the counter that would need a prescription in the UK. They are open during shopping hours; after hours, one in each town remains open all night, the *farmácia de guardia*, and its location is posted in the window of all other *farmácias* and in local newspapers.

Where's the nearest (all-night) chemist? **¿Dónde está la farmácia (de guardia) más cercana?**
I need a doctor/dentist **Necesito un médico/dentista**
sunburn/sunstroke **quemadura del sol/una insolación**
an upset stomach **molestias de estómago**
Is this service public or private? **¿Es este servicio público o privado?**

I

INTERNET

There are a number of internet cafés in Las Palmas, more in Playa del Inglés/Maspalomas, and some in other parts of the island. However, they do tend to come and go, and there are fewer now since Wi-Fi spots have become ubiquitous. In the resorts, you will find them with no trouble in any of the commercial centres. Most places charge around €0.50 for half an hour's access, €1 for an hour. Many are now coin operated.

L

LANGUAGE

The Spanish spoken in the Canary Islands is slightly different from that of the mainland. For instance, islanders don't lisp when they pronounce the letters c or z. A number of Latin American words and expressions are used. The most common are *guagua* (pronounced *wah-wah*), meaning bus, and *papa* (potato). In tourist areas basic English, German and some French is spoken, or at least understood.

The *Berlitz Spanish Phrasebook and Dictionary* covers most of the situations you may encounter in Spain and the Canary Islands.

Do you speak English? **¿Habla usted inglés?**
I don't speak Spanish. **No hablo español.**

M

MAPS

Most tourist offices will give you free maps, which should be sufficient. For something more detailed, go to the official government bookshop, Librería del Cabildo Insular, Calle Cano 24, Las Palmas, tel: 928 381 539; http://libroscanarios.org. Be aware that many road numbers have changed and the ones on the new maps don't always match those on the road signs.

Do you have a map of the city/island? **¿Tiene un plano de la a ciudad/isla?**

MEDIA

Radio and television. Many hotels have satellite tv with several stations in various languages, including CNN. TV Canarias is a local station which includes some English language news and tourist information in its programming. English language radio stations include Kiss FM Live 102.5 MHz, Power FM 98.2 MHz and UK Away FM 99.9 MHz.

Newspapers and periodicals. Major British and Continental newspapers are on sale in the resorts and Las Palmas on the day of publication, as is the European edition of the *New York Herald Tribune*. A number of English-language publications have island news and tourist information, but are not evenly distributed. They include *Holiday Gazette & Tourist Guide* (monthly; http://thegazettelive.com) and various property-based publications.

For Spanish speakers, the island newspapers are *Canarias7* and *La Provincia: Diario de Las Palmas*. Both of these contain listings of events so they can be useful, even if your Spanish is very sketchy. *El País* and other Spanish national newspapers are also available.

MONEY

Currency. The monetary unit in the Canary Islands, as throughout Spain, is the euro, abbreviated €.

Bank notes are available in denominations of €500, 200, 100, 50, 20, 10 and 5. The euro is subdivided into 100 cents and there are coins available for €1 and €2 and for 50, 20, 10, 5, 2 and 1 cent.

Currency exchange. Banks are the preferred place to exchange currency but *casas de cambio* also change money, as do some travel agencies, and these stay open outside banking hours. The larger hotels may also change guests' money, at a slightly less advantageous rate. Banks and exchange offices pay less for cash than

Where's the nearest bank/currency exchange office? **¿Dónde está el banco más cercano/la oficina de cambio más cercana?**
I want to change some dollars/pounds. **Quiero cambiar dólares/libres esterlina.**
Do you accept traveller's cheques? **¿Acepta usted cheques de viajero?**
Can I pay with this credit card? **¿Puedo pagar con esta tarjeta de crédito?**

for traveller's cheques. Always take your passport when you go to change money.

Credit cards. Major international cards are widely recognised, although smaller businesses tend to prefer cash. Visa/Eurocard/MasterCard are most generally accepted. Credit and debit cards, with a PIN number, are also useful for obtaining euros from ATMs – cash machines – which are to be found in all towns and resorts. They offer the most convenient way of obtaining cash and will usually give you the best exchange rate.

Traveller's cheques. Hotels, shops, restaurants and travel agencies all cash traveller's cheques, and so do banks, where you will probably get a better rate. It is safest to cash small amounts at a time, keeping some of your holiday funds in cheques, in the hotel safe.

O

OPENING TIMES

Shops and offices are usually open Monday to Saturday, 10am–1.30pm, 5–8.30pm (although some close on Saturday afternoon). Large supermarkets may stay open all day, as do many shops in the tourist resorts, and some also open on Sunday. Banks usually open Monday to Friday, 8.30am–2pm; post offices Monday to Saturday, 8.30am–2pm.

P

POLICE

There are three police forces in Gran Canaria, as in the rest of Spain. The green-uniformed Guardia Civil (Civil Guard) is the main force. Each town also has its own Policía Municipal (municipal or local police), whose uniform can vary but is mostly blue and grey. The third force, the Cuerpo Nacional de Policía is a national anticrime unit that sports a light brown uniform. All police officers are armed. Spanish police are strict, but courteous to foreign visitors.

National Police: 091
Local Police: 092
Guardia Civil: 062

Where is the nearest police station? **¿Dónde está la comisaría más cercana?**

POST OFFICES

Post offices (www.correos.es) are for mail and telegrams, not telephone calls. The main post office in Las Palmas is at Avenida Primero de Mayo 62; in Playa del Inglés, it is at Edificio Mercurio, Avenida de Tirajana. Stamps *(sellos)* are also sold at tobacconist's *(estanco)* and by most shops selling postcards. Mailboxes are painted yellow. The slot marked *extranjero* is for letters abroad.

Where is the (nearest) post office? **¿Dónde está la oficina de correos (más cercana)?**
A stamp for this letter/postcard, please. **Por favor, un sello para esta carta/tarjeta.**

PUBLIC HOLIDAYS

1 January *Año Nuevo* New Year's Day
6 January *Epifanía* Epiphany
1 May *Día del Trabajo* Labour Day
30 May *Día de las Islas Canarias* Canary Islands' Day
May/June *Corpus Christi* Corpus Christi
16 July *Nuestra Señora del Carmen* Our Lady of Carmen
25 July *Santiago Apóstol* St James' Day
15 August *Asunción* Assumption

12 October *Día de la Hispanidad* Columbus Day
1 November *Todos los Santos* All Saints' Day
6 December *Dia de la Constitución* Constitution Day
8 December *Inmaculada Concepción* Immaculate Conception
25 December *Navidad* Christmas Day
Movable dates:
Carnaval week of Shrove Tuesday/February or early March, depending on the date of Easter
Jueves Santo Maundy Thursday
Viernes Santo Good Friday
Corpus Christi Corpus Christi (early to mid-June)

R

RELIGION

The majority religion is Roman Catholic; church attendance is quite high. Respect people's privacy when visiting churches. There are also Anglican, Muslim, Jewish, Mormon and other religious communities.

T

TAXES

The Impuesto Generalisado Indirecto Canario (IGIC) is levied on all bills at a rate of 7 percent. The tax is not usually included in the price you are quoted for hotel rooms.

TELEPHONES

Phone booths accept coins and cards *(tarjetas telefónicas)*, available from tobacconists; instructions in English and area/country codes are displayed clearly. International calls are expensive, so have a plentiful supply of coins or use a card. *Cabinas* – telephone cabins where you make your call then pay at a desk afterwards – are a more convenient way of making long-distance calls. You will find these in Las Palmas (Parque San Telmo bus station, Parque Santa Catalina and elsewhere) and in commercial centres in the resorts.

Calling directly from your hotel room is expensive unless you are using a card from a local long-distance supplier such as at&t or mci. Get the free connection number applicable to Spain from the supplier before you leave (they are different for each country).

For international calls, wait for the dial tone, then dial 00, wait for a second tone and dial the country code, area code (minus any initial zero) and the number. Country codes are: UK: 44, Ireland: 353, US and Canada: 1, Australia: 61, New Zealand: 64.

International Operator: 025.

Telephone codes for the Canary Islands (which must always be dialled as part of the number, even for local calls): Gran Canaria, Lanzarote and Fuerteventura: 928; Tenerife, El Hierro, La Gomera and La Palma: 922.

TIME ZONES

The time in the Canaries is the same as in the UK, Greenwich Mean Time, but 1 hour behind the rest of Europe, including Spain, and 5 hours ahead of New York. Like the rest of Europe, the islands adopt summer time (putting the clocks forward by an hour) from the end of March through to the end of September.

TIPPING

A service charge is often included in restaurant bills (look for the words *servicio incluído*), so an extra tip is not expected. If it is not included, add around 10 percent, which is also the usual tip for taxi drivers and hairdressers. In bars, customers usually leave a few coins, rounding up the bill. A hotel porter will appreciate €1 for carrying bags to your room; tip hotel maids according to your length of stay.

TOILETS

Toilets in the Canaries are usually called *servicios* or *aseos*. Public conveniences can be found in beach areas and bus stations, and are, for the most part, well-maintained. If using lavatories belonging to bars or restaurants, it is considered polite to buy at least a coffee. Some don't ask questions of casual visitors; other proprietors keep the key behind the bar to make sure their toilets are not used by the general public.

Where are the lavatories? **¿Dónde están los servicios?**

TOURIST INFORMATION

Tourist offices abroad

Canada: 2 Bloor Street West, Suite 3402, Toronto, Ontario M4W 3E2, tel: 1416-961 3131, www.spain.info/en_CA/

Ireland: 1–3 Westmoreland Street, Dublin 2, tel: 01-6350 200

UK: 6th floor, 64 North Row, London W1K 7DE, tel: 020 4675515/13/16, www.tourspain.co.uk, (no personal callers at office).

US: 60 East 42nd Street - Suite 5300 (53rd Floor), New York, NY 10165-0039, tel: 212 265 8822; http://www.spain.info/en_US

Tourist offices in Gran Canaria

Most towns have a tourist office, open during normal business hours. Some of the main ones are:

Las Palmas: Patronato de Turismo, Calle Triana 93, tel: 928 219 600, www.grancanaria.com

Agaete: Calle Nuestra Señora de las Nieves 1, tel: 928 554 382

Agüimes: Plaza de San Antón s/n, tel: 928 124 183

Arucas: Calle León y Castillo 10, tel: 928 623 136

Gáldar: Calle Plaza de Santiago 1, tel: 928 895 855

Maspalomas: Avenida Turoperador Tui, tel: 928 769 585

Playa del Inglés: Yumbo Centre, Avenida EEUU/Avenida España, tel: 928 771 550, www.grancanaria.com

Paseo Marítimo, Centro Comercial Anexo II, tel: 928 768 409
Puerto de Mogán/Puerto Rico: Avenida de Mogán 1, tel: 928 158 804, www.mogan.es
San Agustín: Centro Comercial El Portón, tel: 928 769 262; http://turismo.maspalomas.com.
Tejeda: Calle Leocadio Cabrera s/n, tel: 928 666 189, www.tejeda.es

TRANSPORT

There is no train service but the bus service is cheap and reliable. In Las Palmas, there are two subterranean terminals, in Parque San Telmo and adjacent to Parque Santa Catalina. Tickets on the *guaguas* (buses) cost €1.40. A rechargeable card *BonoGuagua* Sin Contacto (pronounced *bono wawa*) is good value (€8.50) and can be bought in the terminals and in kiosks. City buses run from dawn until 9.30pm, and there's a night service on major routes (tel: 928 305 800, www.guaguas.com).

Long-distance buses leave either from the Parque San Telmo bus station or the Parque Santa Catalina terminal. Buses to the southern resorts are frequent and leave as soon as they are full. They are run by the Global company, which has a centralised information number: tel: 902 381 110; www.globalsu.net. In Playa del Inglés and Maspalomas services are efficient, and run to all the main out-of-town attractions. (For inter-island ferries and flights, see Getting There.)

Taxis. The letters sp (*servicio público*) on the front and rear bumpers of a car indicate that it is a taxi. It may also have a green light in the front windscreen or a green sign indicating '*libre*' when it is free. There is no shortage of taxis in urban areas, and there are usually taxi ranks in the main squares. In towns, the fare is calculated by a meter; for longer, out-of-town journeys there are fixed tariffs, but you may feel happier if you agree an approximate fare in advance. Taxis are good value, with the longest run in Las Palmas costing around €7; from the airport, the fare is around €30. In the southern resorts, where taxis belong to a local co-operative (tel: 928 766 767), it is also a good, inexpensive way to travel.

V

VISAS AND ENTRY REQUIREMENTS

Most visitors, including all EU citizens, the US, Canada, Ireland, Australia and New Zealand, only need a valid passport. No inoculations are required. Although the islands are part of the EU, there is a restriction on duty-free goods that can be brought back to the UK. The allowance is 200 cigarettes, or 50 cigars or 250g tobacco; 1 litre spirits over 22 percent, or 2 litres under 22 percent and 4 litres of wine.

W

WATER

The island suffers from a water shortage, so try not to waste it. It is best to avoid drinking tap water. Bottled water is available everywhere and is inexpensive. *Con gas* is sparkling, *sin gas* is still. Firgas water, produced in the north of the island, is the nicest.

WEBSITES

You can find a lot of useful information online before you start your holiday. Some helpful sites are:

www.grancanaria.com Gran Canaria Patronato de Turismo site.
www.tourspain.es/canarias the Spanish Tourist Office site.
www.spain.info a branch of the official tourist office site.
www.spain-grancanaria.com an excellent general site.
http://canaryzone.com/en travel and hotel guide for the island.
For information on natural parks and rural tourism:
www.ecoturismocanarias.com
www.turismorural.com
www.grancanariarural.com

RECOMMENDED HOTELS

Accommodation in Gran Canaria can roughly be divided into what you will find in the southern resorts and what is available in the rest of the island. In San Agustín, Playa del Inglés and Maspalomas, accommodation is predominantly in large, modern hotels, and many of these are block-booked well in advance by tour companies, although an independent traveller can usually find a room. Puerto Rico is an anomaly in that there are no hotels, only apartments, many of which can only be booked through a travel agent. Puerto de Mogán is unusual in having a small hotel of character. In Las Palmas there is a wide variety of middle- and upper-priced accommodation, much of it near Playa de las Canteras, but good-quality budget accommodation is harder to find. Outside these areas, a number of rural hotels offer comfortable, medium-priced accommodation in attractive old buildings.

Prices given are for two people sharing a double room in high season. Breakfast is usually included in hotels in the top three brackets; tax (IGIC) at 5 percent is extra (prices are an approximate guide only).

€€€€	above 180 euros
€€€	100–180 euros
€€	65–100 euros
€	below 65 euros

LAS PALMAS

AC-Gran Canaria €€–€€€ *Calle Eduardo Benot 3-5, tel: 928 266 100*, http://achotels.marriott.com. This 25-storey hotel, close to Parque Santa Catalina, has 227 functional rooms. Ask for one on an upper floor: you get a great view, the rooftop pool and restaurant are closer, and the traffic noise is less disturbing. Geared more towards business travellers and those on short city breaks.

Hotel Verol €, *Calle Sagasta 25, tel: 928 262 104*, www.hotelverol.com. A modern hotel situated between Parque Santa Catalina and the beach. There are 25 basic, clean and comfortable room. Here, you will get good value for your money.

Madrid €, *Plazoleta de Cairasco 4, tel: 928 360 664*, www.elhotelma drid.com. In a pretty little square in Triana, the Madrid has a long history and bags of atmosphere, which more than compensate for the somewhat old-fashioned facilities. It is a popular hotel, so book in advance. Rooms facing the square can be noisy in the evenings. No breakfast.

Parque €–€€ *Muelle de Las Palmas 2, tel: 928 368 000*, http://hotel parqueenlaspalmas.com. It is not a beautiful building but rooms are comfortable and it has a very convenient, central location, right beside Parque San Telmo bus terminal, not far from Vegueta. There is a rooftop restaurant, a sauna and steam room. There are suites, single, double and triple rooms. Good value.

Pensión Sea of Clouds € *Calle Nicolás Estévanez 31, tel: 928 263 123*. www.pensionibiza com. One of the least expensive pensions in Las Palmas, the main draw is its proximity to the beach. It looks a bit dingy from the outside but rooms are functional. Only few have private bathrooms. No credit cards.

Reina Isabel €€€, *Calle Alfredo L. Jones 40, tel: 928 260 100*, www. bullhotels.com. Smartly renovated, and with an excellent location on Playa de las Canteras, the Reina Isabel is a smart and reliably good place to stay. There is a rooftop pool and a gym, and the Summum restaurant is widely recommended.

Santa Catalina €€€€, *Parque Doramas, Calle León y Castillo 227, tel: 928 243 040*, www.hotelsantacatalina.com. Set in a lush park and founded in 1890, this is the oldest, grandest and most expensive hotel in town. Rooms are furnished with antiques; there's a casino, convention facilities, a beautiful spa centre, and an excellent restaurant. Staying here would be an unforgettable experience.

Sercotel Cristina Las Palmas €€€ *Calle Gomera 6, tel: 933 636 363*, www.hotelcristinalaspalmas.com. Right on the beach, the largest hotel in town with 306 rooms has all the extras expected of a five-star, including a large pool, cocktail bar, restaurants, a disco and parking. Definitely not a place for those looking for a calm and relaxing break.

AGÜIMES

Escuela Rural Casa de los Camellos €€ *Calle El Progreso 12, tel: 928 785 003*, www.hecansa.com. An attractive *turismo rural* hotel built around a shady courtyard, with 12 traditionally furnished en suite rooms. Run by HECANSA, the Canaries official hotel and restaurant organisation. There is a good restaurant and bar and the staff are friendly and helpful. There are bikes to rent and packed lunches can be made if required.

SANTA BRÍGIDA

Hotel Escuela Santa Brígida €€€ *Calle Real de Coello 2, tel: 928 478 400*, www.hecansa.com. Another member of the prestigious HECANSA chain. The service is excellent and rooms are large and well equipped. There is a pool in pleasant gardens, a gym, sauna and fine restaurant. Close to Las Palmas and to the Bandama Golf Club. Good deals available (Friday–Saturday nights).

Hotel Bandama Golf €€ *Lugar de Golf 14, tel: 928 351 538*, www.bandamagolfhotel.com. Quite small, with just 25 rooms, this is the place for golfers. Tennis and horse riding are also on offer, or just enjoy the pool and the scenery. All rooms have either terrace or balcony. Special packages for four-day stays with green fees.

MASPALOMAS

Riu Palace Oasis €€€€ *Plaza de las Palmeras 2, tel: 928 141 448*, www.riu.com. This is one of the most luxurious hotels on the island, set in a palm grove just a few metres from the dunes. Beautiful gardens, pools, putting green, tennis courts, billiard room, gym and sauna.

Seaside Grand Hotel Residencia €€€€ *Avenida del Oasis 32, tel: 928 723 100;* www.grand-hotel-residencia.es. This exclusive hotel consists of traditional-style villas and suites. Set in a palm grove 200m/

yds from the dunes, it feels removed from the hubbub of Maspalomas. Attractive tropical gardens, gym and thalassotherapy centre.

Seaside Palm Beach €€€, *Avenida del Oasis, tel: 928 721 032*, www.hotel-palm-beach.es. This stylish seven-storey hotel has individually designed rooms. All rooms have balconies, and there are four restaurants, a palm garden and spa facilities and treatments. Located a few metres from the beach.

PLAYA DEL INGLÉS

Bohemia Suites & Spa €€€€, *Avenida Estados Unidos 28, tel: 928 563 4008*; http://bohemia-grancanaria.com. In a rather noisy location, but close to the beach, it's a luxury oasis with many facilities including a spa, wellness area, pool, top-floor lounge and a restaurant with a panoramic view of the Maspalomas dunes. Adults only.

Eugenia Victoria €€ *Avenida de Gran Canaria 26, tel: 928 762 500*, www.bullhotels.com. Nine storeys high with marble foyer, this hotel has large, pleasant rooms, a wellness centre, large pool, vast breakfasts, children's entertainment and rather impersonal service. About 15 minutes' walk to the beach but there's a frequent, free bus. Five-night minimum stay.

IFA Buenaventura €€ *Calle Gánigo 6, tel: 928 761 650/902 450 010*, www.lopesan.com. One of the island's biggest hotels, with 724 rooms, all with balconies. Ten minutes' walk from the centre, but there's a free bus to the beach six times a day. Two pools, six restaurants serving a wide variety of food, entertainment including karaoke, a gym, three tennis courts and a variety of sports activities.

IFA Continental €€ *Avenida de Italia 2, tel: 928 760 033/902 450 010*, www.lopesan.com. Popular with families – it has a 'mini-club' during school holidays – this hotel set in gardens has a pool, sauna, solarium and massage, plus a volleyball/basketball court and disco.

Parque Tropical €€€ *Avenida de Italia 1, tel: 928 774 012/928 774 016*, www.hotelparquetropical.com. This is a modern hotel but constructed in traditional, local style in a quiet location. There is a pleasant garden and pool, tennis, table tennis, sauna and hairdressing salon.

Riu Don Miguel €€ *Avenida de Tirajana 30, tel: 928 761 508*, www.riu.com. It looks functional, but this is a comfortable hotel with 250 rooms. Centrally located but 10 minutes' walk from the beach (free bus service). Tennis, volleyball and billiards plus playground, pool and entertainment. Adults only. Three-night minimum stay.

Sentido Gran Canaria Princess €€€ *Avenida de Gran Canaria 18, tel: 928 768 132*, www.princess-hotels.com. This seven-storey hotel, 10 minutes' walk from the beach, has big, light rooms, all with balconies. There's a vast pool, two tennis courts and a sauna. Good out-of-season price reductions. Adults only and two-night minimum stay in high season.

PUERTO DE MOGÁN

Hotel The Puerto de Mogán €€ *Club de Mar, Urb. Puerto de Mogán, tel: 928 565 066*, www.hotelpuertodemogan.com. This pretty little hotel is right on the quayside, so the comfortably furnished rooms have views over the sea and beach or over the port. Friendly atmosphere, lots of personal touches, a small pool and a pleasant restaurant. The hotel also rents attractive apartments dotted around the harbour, some with roof terraces.

Pensión Eva € *Marinero 65, tel: 928 565 235*. There are few *pensións* on the coast, so this is worth a mention. It's a cheerful little place 800m/yards from the beach, offering shared bathroom, a communal kitchen and laundry facilities.

SAN AGUSTÍN

Gloria Palace San Agustin Thalasso & Hotel €€–€€€ *Calle Las Margaritas s/n, tel: 928 128 500*, www.gloriapalaceth.com. This smart hotel has a poolside bar, tennis courts, mini-golf, a children's playground, a disco, a thalassotherapy centre and an à la carte restaurant. About 600m/yds from the beach.

Hotel Dunas Don Gregory €€€ *Calle de las Dalias 11, tel: 928 773 877*, www.hotelesdunas.com. A large modern four-star hotel (with 199 rooms and 14 suites) which has all the usual facilities, and is right by the beach and opposite the shopping centre. All-inclusive terms available.

Meliá Tamarindos €€€, *Calle Retama 3, tel: 928 774 090*, www.melia. com. The wide range of sports facilities at this luxurious hotel includes tennis, squash, volleyball and archery. There are also boutiques and conference facilities and one of only two casinos on the island, with everything you need for a spell of indulgence. Half-board terms available.

THE WEST AND NORTH

AGAETE

Finca Las Longueras €€, *Valle de Agaete, tel: 928 898 145*, www.las longueras.com. At the bottom of a dirt track off the main road between Agaete and Los Barrazales, this rust-coloured 19th-century mansion has been converted into a beautiful *casa rural*. There are nine carefully furnished en suite rooms, a separate apartment and new junior suites with great views. There is a small pool, and good, Canarian food is served in a tranquil setting.

ARUCAS

La Hacienda del Buen Suceso €€€, *Carretera Arucas–Bañaderos Km1, tel: 928 622 945*, www.haciendabuensuceso.com. This rural hotel set in a banana plantation just outside town is a fine place to relax. It has 18 rooms, each individually furnished with antiques and with comfortable sofas on shady balconies. There is a pretty courtyard and garden, a small heated swimming pool, a steam room and jacuzzi, and a large barbecue area as well as a pleasant restaurant using lots of local produce.

GÁLDAR

Hotel Hacienda de Anzo €€ *Calle Pablo Díaz 37, tel: 928 551 655*; www. hotelhaciendadeanzo.es. In a valley about 1km (0.5 mile) to the north of Gáldar and about 3km (2 miles) from Sardina beach, this attractive three-star in a typical country house is set amid gardens and has just six pleasant rooms.

CRUZ DE TEJEDA

El Refugio €€ *Cruz de Tejeda s/n, tel: 928 666 513*, www.hotelruralelrefugio.com. A wonderful place to relax after walking in the Roque Nublo rural park, with a swimming pool and a sauna for tired bones. Just 10 rooms, comfortably furnished, and there's a good restaurant, too.

Parador Hotel de Cruz de Tejeda €€€ *Cruz de Tejeda s/n, tel: 928 012 500*, www.parador.es. Now reopened after years of restoration work, with all the comfort and good taste associated with the Parador chain. The excellent restaurant even offers a gluten-free menu. And, of course, the views are wonderful.

FATAGA

Molino de Agua €€, *Carretera Fataga–San Bartolomé Km45, tel: 928 071 084*; www.elmolinodeagua.com. A small rural hotel in a palm grove, close to the restored mill from which it gets its name, this is a peaceful, pleasing place. The restaurant serves authentic local dishes; excursions can be arranged if required.

SAN BARTOLOMÉ DE TIRAJANA

Las Tirajanas €€€€ *Calle Oficial Mayor José Rubio s/n, tel: 928 566 969*, www.hotel-lastirajanas.com. A modern, tastefully decorated hotel overlooking the Barranco de Tirajana. Has a heated pool, jacuzzi and sauna, a restaurant serving authentic Canarian food, and all the facilities you would expect of a four-star hotel, plus peace and quiet and splendid views.

VEGA DE SAN MATEO

Hotel Rural Las Calas €€€ *Calle El Arenal 36, San Mateo, tel: 928 661 436*, www.hotelrurallascalas.com. Just 3km (2 miles) outside Vega de San Mateo this small hotel offers tranquillity and comfort. Set in lovely grounds, with a vegetable garden that provides produce for the restaurant, it has nine individually designed rooms. It makes a good base for exploring Tejeda/Roque Nublo.

CASAS RURALES

For a wider selection of rural houses for rent, contact Gran Canaria Rural: www.grancanariarural.com (also see Accommodation, page 114) or www.casitascanarias.com. Price categories given here are per night for two people but are often lower for stays of a week or more. The minimum stay is usually two nights.

€€€	over 95 euros
€€	75–95 euros
€	under 75 euros

AGÜIMES

Casa de las Suárez €€ *Plaza de Santo Domingo, tel: 928 124 183, (rural tourism office).* Attractive stone house in a pretty square, traditionally furnished. Has solar-heated water, three double bedrooms, two bathrooms. No Internet, adults only. Seven-night minimum stay.

Casa del Cura €€ *Calle Moral, tel: 928 124 183 (rural tourism office).* Traditional Canarian house in the town centre with two double bedrooms, two bathrooms and a garden.

MOYA

Casa Nanita €€ *Camino de la esperanza 38, Fontanales, tel: 928 464 464.* Three separate self-contained units in a rural *finca* 9km (5 miles) from Moya. Swimming pool, garden and barbecue. Bikes available.

TEROR

Casa Rural Doña Margarita €€ *Calle Padre Cueto 4, tel: 928 631 921,* www.margaritacasarural.com. Opposite the Palacio Episcopal, this refurbished 18th-century house comprises three separate units, each with two bedrooms and well-equipped kitchens. Special (higher) rates during the fiesta, in the first two weeks in September. Tranquil and highly recommended.

APARTMENTS AND BUNGALOWS **141**

APARTMENTS AND BUNGALOWS

Price categories are per night for two people in high season but there are good deals to be had at other times. Only a small selection is given, as many can only be booked through a travel agent:

€€€ over 95 euros
€€ 75–95 euros
€ under 75 euros

LAS PALMAS

Bajamar € *Calle Venezuela 34, tel: 928 276 254,* www.hotelaparta mentoslaspalmas.com. Located a couple of blocks back from Las Canteras beach, this modern block has four types of spacious, comfortable apartment, with all mod-cons.

Brisamar Canteras €€ *Paseo de las Canteras 49, tel: 928 269 400,* www.brisamarcanteras.com. Right on the beach, it offers 45 apartments, some with sea view terraces, and shared gardens.

Colón Playa €–€€ *Calle Alfredo L. Jones 45, tel: 928 265 954,* www. apartamentoscolonplaya.com. Situated on the beach, many of the 42 studio apartments have a balcony and sea view.

THE SOUTH

MASPALOMAS
Eó Suite Hotel Jardín Dorado €€ *Avenida Touroperador Tjaerborg 6, tel: 928 767 950;* www.eohotels.es. This large, luxurious complex has 114 bungalows, as well as pools, a gym and tennis centre. There are special rates at the adjoining golf course for guests.

Maspalomas Oasis Club €€, *Avenida Air Marín s/n, tel: 928 145 555,* www.maspalomasoasisclub.com. A complex of 100 bungalows set amid gardens, with basic, clean rooms. Includes a volleyball court and children's playground.

PLAYA DEL INGLÉS
Servatur Barbados €€ *Avenida de Tirajana 17–19, tel: 928 760 426;*

www.servaturhotels.com. Sixty-eight apartments in two adjoining buildings in a very central location, which means it is busy and can be noisy. There is a pool and gardens, a bar and a restaurant.

PUERTO DE MOGÁN
La Venecia de Canarias €€ *Urb. Puerto de Mogán, Local 328, tel: 928 565 600*, www.laveneciadecanarias.net. An enticing little complex near the marina. Well-furnished apartments with good kitchens.

PUERTO RICO
Apartamentos El Greco €€ *Avenida Olímpicos Doreste y Molina 38, tel: 928 560 356*; www.elgrecopuertorico.com. Attractively designed apartments and bungalows, close to the beach, with a good restaurant. Mainly booked by tour operators, so contact a UK travel agent.

Apartamentos Lufesa €€, *Avenida Tomás Roca Bosch 10, tel: 928 561 225*; www.lufesa.org. Forty-two pleasant apartments in the town, so there is no need to climb the hill. Part of the small Sunsuites chain.

Apartamentos Mayagüez € *Avenida Lanzarote 22, tel: 928 561 611*; www.apartamentosmayaguez.es. A small complex close to the sea on the Puerto Nuevo side, set in gardens with a pool.

SAN AGUSTÍN
Buganvilla € *Calle Los Jazmines 17, tel: 928 760 300*; www.apartamentos buganvilla.com. Twenty-four modern boutique apartments with views over the beach. Four-night minimum stay.

Sunsuites Carolina €€€ *Calle Cardones 3, tel: 928 778 200*; www.sun suites.es. Pretty whitewashed apartments with terraces, pool and lush gardens, close to the beach.

THE NORTH

AGAETE
Apartamentos El Angosto €, *Calle Obispo Pildain 11, tel: 928 554 192*, www.elangosto.eu. Peaceful location; 12 attractive apartments, set in pleasant gardens, with pool, restaurant and sea and mountain views. There are not many apartments in the north, so this one is a good find.

INDEX

Berlitz POCKET GUIDE

GRAN CANARIA

Fifth Edition 2016

Editor: Carine Tracanelli
Author: Pam Barrett
Head of Production: Rebeka Davies
Picture Editor: Tom Smyth
Cartography Update: Carte
Update Production: AM Services
Photography Credits: 100 Montaditos
6MC; Alamy 6TL, 7, 95; Carmencabrera.
info 41; Fotolia 70; Gary John Norman/Apa
Publications 34; Getty Images 4TC, 4MC, 5MC,
6TL, 7M, 13, 14, 15, 19, 21, 24, 30, 38, 43, 45,
47, 49, 51, 55, 61, 64, 68, 74, 88, 92, 97, 102;
Gran Canaria Tourist Board 32, 37, 44, 52, 59,
78, 84, 87; Gran Canaria-info.com 63; Gregory
Wrona/Apa Publications 36, 77; iStock 5M,
7T, 8L, 11, 26, 73, 90, 98; Lucy Johnston 100;
Musee Nestor 35; Pam Barrett 69; Public
domain 16; Shutterstock 4ML, 4TL, 5T, 5TC,
5M, 5MC, 6ML, 6ML, 8R, 9, 9R, 22, 23, 28, 48,
54, 57, 58, 66, 76, 80, 82
Cover Picture: 4Corners Images

Distribution

UK, Ireland and Europe: Apa Publications
(UK) Ltd; sales@insightguides.com
United States and Canada: Ingram Publisher
Services; ips@ingramcontent.com
Australia and New Zealand: Woodslane;
info@woodslane.com.au
Southeast Asia: Apa Publications (SN) Pte;
singaporeoffice@insightguides.com
Hong Kong, Taiwan and China:
Apa Publications (HK) Ltd;
hongkongoffice@insightguides.com
Worldwide: Apa Publications (UK) Ltd;
sales@insightguides.com

**Special Sales, Content Licensing
and CoPublishing**
Insight Guides can be purchased in bulk
quantities at discounted prices. We can create
special editions, personalised jackets and
corporate imprints tailored to your needs.
sales@insightguides.com;
www.insightguides.biz

Contact us
Every effort has been made to provide
accurate information in this publication,
but changes are inevitable. The publisher
cannot be responsible for any resulting loss,
inconvenience or injury. We would appreciate
it if readers would call our attention to any
errors or outdated information. We also
welcome your suggestions; please contact us
at: berlitz@apaguide.co.uk
www.insightguides.com/berlitz

Berlitz Trademark Reg. U.S. Patent Office
and other countries. Marca Registrada.
Used under licence from the Berlitz
Investment Corporation